OSPREY COMBAT AIRCRAFT • 92

P-47 THUNDERBOLT
UNITS OF THE TWELFTH
AIR FORCE

SERIES EDITOR: TONY HOLMES

OSPREY COMBAT AIRCRAFT • 92

P-47 THUNDERBOLT UNITS OF THE TWELFTH AIR FORCE

JONATHAN BERNSTEIN

OSPREY
PUBLISHING

Front Cover
Lt Ray Knight of the 346th Fighter Squadron (FS)/350th Fighter Group (FG) banks sharply to avoid 20 mm flak as he streaks over Bergamo airfield, near Milan in northern Italy, in his P-47D on 25 April 1945. Leading a flight of four Thunderbolts, Knight was on his third airfield strafing mission (the second to Bergamo) in 48 hours. The principal targets during these attacks were Luftwaffe aircraft that were being readied for a counter-offensive against Allied forces that had just crossed the Po River.

Over a two-day period, Knight singlehandedly destroyed 20 German aeroplanes on the ground, and his flight accounted for many more.

Despite taking several hits, Knight pressed home his attack in the face of withering flak, thus ensuring the destruction of yet another Ju 88 on his final pass over Bergamo. Knowing that his unit was already facing a shortage of operational aircraft, Knight elected to fly his P-47 back to Pisa rather than bail out over friendly territory. However, crossing the Appenines, he began to lose altitude. As he made an approach to belly land his aeroplane, the P-47's wingtip clipped a tree, causing it to cartwheel and explode.

For his fearless actions on 24-25 April 1945, leading a flight of four Thunderbolts against overwhelming flak to destroy a significant number of Luftwaffe aircraft in northern Italy, thus breaking up a German air counter-offensive, Lt Ray Knight was posthumously awarded the Medal of Honor (*Cover artwork by Mark Postlethwaite*)

Title pages
Due to the Thunderbolt's poor forward visibility when taxiing, the aeroplane's crew chief often rode on the wing while the P-47 taxied out to the runway to warn the pilot of any obstacles ahead. *ANGELPUSS II*, Lt Louis Barnett's assigned aircraft, taxies in at Fano, after a successful mission. The P-47D-27/28 (serial unknown) assigned to the 79th FG's 86th FS, had just returned from supporting British troops over the Eighth Army Front (*Dave Hoover Collection*)

First published in Great Britain in 2012 by Osprey Publishing
Midland House, West Way, Botley, Oxford, OX2 0PH
44-02 23rd Street, Suite 219, Long Island City, NY, 11101, USA

E-mail; info@ospreypublishing.com
Osprey Publishing is part of the Osprey Group
© 2012 Osprey Publishing Limited

A CIP catalogue record for this book is available from the British Library

ISBN: 978 1 84908 672 1
E-book ISBN: 978 1 84908 673 8

Edited by Tony Holmes
Page design by Tony Truscott
Cover Artwork by Mark Postlethwaite
Aircraft Profiles by Chris Davey
Index by Michael Forder
Originated by United Graphic Pte Ltd
Printed in China through Bookbuilders

12 13 14 15 16   10 9 8 7 6 5 4 3 2 1

Osprey Publishing is supporting the Woodland Trust, the UK's leading woodland conservation charity by funding the dedication of trees.

www.ospreypublishing.com

ACKNOWLEDGEMENTS
I would like to thank Doug Patteson, Mark O'Boyle, Jim Selders, Dave Hoover, Tyler Emery, Mark Barry, Keith Vizcarra, Cesar Campiani Maximiano (for the 1st BFS photos and information) and Don Kaiser for the use of their images. To the Air Force Historical Services Office at Bolling AFB I owe a major debt of gratitude – thanks Yvonne Kinkaid and Terry Kiss. I would also like to thank historians Syd Edwards and Nigel Julian, whose suggestions and opinions I value greatly, and Luftwaffe specialist Nick Beale. My wonderful wife Katie and our two beautiful sons Julian and Jack never failed to inspire me throughout this project! My sincere thanks to our parents Dorrie and Jeff Bernstein and Ginny and Paul Dyson too for all you've done for us while I've been working on this book. And, finally, thank you to my grandfather, who helped me understand what it was like to be an infantryman scrambling for cover under enemy fire, and the sudden elation of hearing the sound of those beautiful P-47 Thunderbolts overhead. Papa, I miss you tons.

CONTENTS

ORIGINS OF THE AMERICAN FIGHTER-BOMBER

Although the Mediterranean Theatre of Operations (MTO) has been overshadowed by the greater scope of combat seen in the European Theatre, many developments in Allied doctrine had their origins in North Africa and the MTO well before Allied troops set foot on the European continent. The combat environments found in North Africa, Sicily and Italy often saw air power become the decisive tool for mission accomplishment, and therefore served as the testing ground for innovation in tactics and doctrine that would become standard as the war progressed.

US Army Air Force (USAAF) doctrine was still rather nebulous when the 57th FG's P-40Fs took off from the deck of USS *Ranger* (CV 4), sailing near the African Gold Coast, in July 1942. The role air power was to play in North Africa was anything but certain, and it was not until the 57th (and subsequent P-40 groups that followed) gained significant experience operating alongside its British allies that a doctrine began to emerge. The newly formed Desert Air Force (DAF), comprised of units from the US Ninth Air Force and RAF squadrons, was the primary aerial support for Allied ground units in North Africa. P-40Fs in-theatre were modified to carry a 500-lb bomb on the centreline rack and three 30-lb fragmentation bomblets under each wing.

Air superiority is an essential element of any aviation operation. In North Africa, although General Erwin Rommel's *Afrika Korps* was retreating, Luftwaffe fighters remained a significant threat to DAF bomber units through to early 1943. Allied aircraft needed to get to their targets with minimal threat from enemy fighters. In order to accomplish this, escort fighters, logistics and significant planning and coordination was needed. The employment of fighter types as fighter-bombers also helped defeat the Jagdwaffe.

Using DAF fighters both as a covering force and as the attackers enabled a greater flexibility in ordnance delivery, and also in the ability to defend against enemy

P-40Fs of the 324th and 57th FGs await their next mission at an Advanced Landing Ground in the North African desert. When the USA entered the war, fighter-bombers did not exist in the USAAF, but quick lessons in the North African desert with excellent RAF instructors taught many of those early aviators the skills they needed as they became squadron and group commanders flying P-47s in 1944 (*Author's collection*)

fighters attempting to shoot down the attacking force. Once fighter-bomber pilots had dropped their ordnance, they would be able to defend themselves as they fought their way back to friendly lines.

DAF P-40 groups performed well in North Africa, using the aircraft's improved manoeuvrability at lower altitudes to effectively combat the faster Bf 109. Their contribution to the war effort was instrumental in solidifying doctrine that had been postulated by air power proponents for the preceding two decades. Actions like the 'Palm Sunday Massacre' of 18 April 1943, when P-40s from the 57th and 324th FGs claimed 76 German aircraft (mainly Ju 52/3ms) destroyed, proved decisive in the overall defeat of Axis forces in North Africa by 12 May 1943.

Published doctrine caught up to practice shortly after the North African victory. The introduction of *Field Manual FM100-20 Command and Employment of Air Power* in July 1943 laid out the doctrinal priorities for combat aviation, and for the first time put air forces on an equal footing with army ground forces. The establishment of USAAF doctrine set the support of friendly ground forces by air as a third priority, behind seizing air superiority and disrupting the enemy's infrastructure through bombardment and interdicting his logistics chain. While fighter-bombers assisted in maintaining air superiority when the opportunity arose, interdiction and close air support (CAS) were the primary function of tactical air force units.

In mid 1943, the USAAF order of battle in the North African theatre underwent a significant reorganisation. Headquarters, Ninth Air Force was reassigned to the European Theatre of Operations (ETO) as the core of the new tactical air force in the UK, turning its fighter groups over to the newly created Twelfth Air Force as the new tactical air force in the MTO. Along with this reorganisation, the Fifteenth Air Force was created in the autumn of 1943 as the MTO's strategic air arm.

As the North African campaign came to a close and the Allies advanced across the Mediterranean, newer fighter types saw their introduction to combat. The most significant of these was the North American A-36 Apache, an Allison-engined dive-bomber variant of the not-yet-famous P-51. A lethal machine optimised for air-to-ground work, the A-36 was a fast aircraft even with a full load of two 500-lb bombs. Making its combat debut over Sicily with the 27th FG in June 1943, the Apache impressed those that flew it thanks to the aircraft's manoeuvrability, speed and heavy armament of six 0.50-cal machine

While the P-40F/L was the predominant fighter-bomber in the Mediterranean from 1942 through to mid-1944, the A-36A Apache (the dive-bomber version of the P-51A Mustang) proved an incredibly capable machine in the hands of 27th and 86th FG pilots. The aircraft's combat career was doomed, however, by a small production run, scarcity of spare parts and the fact that manufacturer North American quickly fitted the Rolls-Royce Merlin engine into the Mustang airframe in place of the A-36's Allison. These 526th FS Apaches are fuelled, armed and ready for their next combat mission over the Italian Front (*Dave Hoover Collection*)

guns. Indeed, this weaponry made the Apache one of the most heavily armed single-engined aircraft in the inventory to date – only the new Thunderbolt carried more firepower.

The A-36 soldiered on with both the 27th and 86th FGs into early 1944. However, its short production run of only 500 airframes made conditions very difficult for the groups' maintainers. Keeping an adequate supply of spare parts available became progressivly harder, and according to several sources, a coin was flipped to see which group would lose its Apaches and transition to a new airframe. The 27th lost out and in February 1944 began handing its A-36s over to the 86th FG while converting to hand-me-down P-40s from the 57th FG. The group would fly these war weary aircraft for just a few short months, however, as it transitioned to newer P-47s in May.

A NEW MISSION

When the Republic P-47 began arriving in-theatre in September 1943 through North African ports, it was intended for use as a high altitude interceptor. The turbo-supercharged Pratt & Whitney R-2800 radial engine gave the fighter excellent high altitude performance, which was a feature lacking in both the P-40 and A-36 that left them at a serious disadvantage when engaging the Bf 109G. The Thunderbolt also had a greater range than other single-engined fighters in the MTO, allowing it to escort USAAF heavy bombers almost as far as the P-38 Lightning.

The first MTO unit to convert to the new fighter was the 325th FG, beginning in September 1943. It took just short of a month to convert the group from the P-40, and during that time the 325th was transferred from the Twelfth to the Fifteenth Air Force to provide fighter escorts for strategic bombing missions over Germany. Due to changes in higher headquarters and in airframes, the 325th did not fly its first combat mission in the P-47D until 4 December.

Pilots of the 325th FG gather under the wing of P-47D 42-76021 soon after they had commenced flying the Thunderbolt. Although the 325th did not fly Thunderbolts as part of the Twelfth Air Force, many of its aeroplanes subsequently did after being transferred out of the group. Capt Lewis 'Bill' Chick of the 325th shot down two Bf 109s in this aeroplane before turning it over to the 86th FG, with whom it soldiered on through 1944 (*Author's collection*)

Final assembly of the first P-47s arriving in-theatre took place in Tunisia, after which the aircraft were assigned to an operational unit. Here, two technicians are securing the fighter's ammunition bays as the latest batch awaits their tail feathers. The F-6C tactical reconnaissance Mustang coded CD (42-103014) to the right of the P-47s is from the 111th TRS. Photographed in January 1944, this was probably one of the first Merlin-engined P-51s to arrive in the MTO (*Author's collection*)

While not the aeroplane he scored his final two kills in, Al Froning flew this P-47D 42-75648 for the remainder of his tour, and had all six of his victories painted on the side of it. Froning scored four kills in the P-40F, including two Ju 52/3ms in the famous 'Palm Sunday Massacre'. The 57th FG claimed 74 enemy aircraft shot down and a nearly equal number of probables for the loss of six Warhawks during this one-sided clash on 18 April 1943 (*Bob Hanning collection via 57thfightergroup.com/Mark O'Boyle*)

While the Thunderbolt's service with the 325th was limited to six months as part of the Fifteenth Air Force, the aeroplanes it flew would be extremely important to Twelfth Air Force fighter units in the months that followed.

Shortly after the 325th began its conversion onto the new fighter, the 57th FG followed, getting its first P-47s a few days after Thanksgiving and flying its first combat mission the day after the 325th on 5 December 1943. The group's three squadrons (64th, 65th and 66th FSs) each contributed three P-47s and four P-40s to escort a force of 36 B-25s returning from an attack on Split harbour, in Yugoslavia. One P-47 developed engine trouble and returned early, but the remaining eight Thunderbolts arrived at the bomber rendezvous point and patrolled over Split. There was no contact with either enemy aircraft or the B-25s.

Although this particular mission was a standard bomber escort, December had ushered in a new phase of operations targeting Axis shipping in the Adriatic that would eventually capitalise on the P-47's ordnance-carrying capabilities. These first missions focused on maritime reconnaissance and interdiction along the Dalmatian coast, and on 16 December the 57th drew first blood with its new mounts.

The group's 1000th mission since its P-40Fs left the deck of *Ranger* was a fighter sweep over the Peljesac peninsula, on the Yugoslavian coast. A mixed formation of eight P-47s from all three squadrons departed Amendola airfield, in Italy, at 0900 hrs and headed northeast across the Adriatic Sea – one aircraft had engine trouble and was forced to abort. After dead reckoning nearly 120 miles over open water, the formation reached land just west of Zabrde and strafed a number of targets between there and Ston (three miles to the south) in support of Yugoslavian partisans, starting fires among a grouping of supply sheds. Flying line abreast, all eight P-47s then turned northeast towards Drace, looking for additional targets of opportunity.

While pulling up from strafing buildings north of Drace, the fighters were bounced by a flight of at least eight Bf 109G-6s from IV./JG 27, led by Leutnant Wolfgang Lang. The P-47 pilots turned into their attackers and went on the offensive, despatching four Messerschmitts and driving the rest off. The dogfight had taken place over the eastern Mediterranean, and ranged from near zero altitude up to 1000 ft. 1Lt (later Capt) Alfred Froning claimed two Bf 109s, bringing his personal total to six (four kills while flying P-40Fs) and making him the 65th's second ace.

In his debrief, 1Lt Froning recounted;

'I was leading the top flight of three P-47s. We had just pulled up from strafing "Stone" [sic] and were at 1000 ft. 1Lt Monahan called in one snapper and attacked same. As he dove on the enemy aircraft, a second Me 109 closed on his tail. I was above and behind him, and closed in for a dead astern shot at a range of 250 yards. I opened fire and observed pieces and smoke trail off his Me 109. The enemy pilot tried to pull up and I continued firing. He then half rolled at 900 ft and went straight into the water burning. As I broke away, two cannon shells hit my right wing, causing my right wheel to drop and set the wing on fire. I tried turning, but my ship was crippled, resulting in my tail getting shot up. I hit the deck, trying to evade the Me 109's fire.

'Immediately, two more Me 109s jumped me. The three of them then ran a gunnery pattern on me from line abreast astern. I took hits all over the aircraft. Two of the Me 109s left, while the remaining ship turned onto the tail of another P-47 that crossed our path. I turned about and fired a 30-degree deflection shot, gradually closing it down to line astern. I observed approximately three or four feet of his left wing fly off, as well as the balance of his tail section. He was throwing out much white and black smoke. He was at 400 ft and started to roll over on his back in a 60-degree dive. When last seen, he was at 150 ft, apparently out of control on his back, smoking. This aircraft was observed to crash into the sea.'

1Lt Monahan had better luck, claiming two without being hit;

'Upon completion of our strafing attack, three of us saw 15+ Me 109s. I attacked one flying on the deck. He did a chandelle up to the left and I followed, shooting all the time. Smoke began to pour from him when 400 ft above the sea. Looking back, I saw him crash into the sea. I then sighted one on my left and did a 90-degree turn, firing a long burst at close range. I then had to break off as another Me 109 was closing in on me. I turned into him but did not engage. I then looked to my right and saw the Me 109 that I had previously engaged go down in smoke and crash. The pilot bailed out.'

1Lt Harold Monahan was also credited with two Bf 109s destroyed. After the engagement, the flight turned north toward Trpanj and then back across the Adriatic. 1Lt Froning's P-47 was fairly well shot up, but was able to coax it back to Amendola with the rest of the flight. The fighter's ability to keep flying despite numerous cannon hits was clearly evident, and a trait that Thunderbolt pilots would come to rely on in future months.

A second mission launched from Amendola shortly after the 0900 hrs flight had engaged a similar force of Bf 109s just south and east of 1Lt Froning's flight. 66th FS pilots, flying P-40Fs, brought down an additional three Messerschmitts confirmed, one probable and three damaged. The 57th flew a third mission later that day with a mixed force of P-40s and P-47s. Again looking for maritime targets along the Peljesac peninsula, the P-47s provided top cover for the group's P-40s, which were strafing targets between Viganj and Orebic. The Thunderbolts' guns were silent, but the flight's Warhawks attacked several troop concentrations, knocked out two machine gun emplacements and destroyed a locomotive pulling seven rail cars before heading for home.

Capt Al Froning climbs out of his P-47 after another successful mission. Froning was the only 57th FG pilot to 'make ace' while flying the Thunderbolt, claiming two Bf 109s on 16 January 1944 to add to his quartet of kills in the P-40F (*Bob Hanning collection via 57thfightergroup.com/Mark O'Boyle*)

The following day, the mixed-squadron formation of eight P-47s and 12 P-40s took off on another shipping interdiction mission. On their inbound leg, flying at 10,000 ft, the P-47 element surprised a flight of five Bf 109s and attacked line abreast from almost dead astern, destroying two immediately and shooting the tail off of a third that attempted to manoeuvre. Lt Liebing of the 64th FS was the first to draw blood;

'One of them made the mistake of lagging behind, so I snuck up to where I could get a shot at him. I got him in my sights for a 60-degree deflection shot. I saw the tracers going out toward him. He seemed to fly right into them, and all of a sudden he wasn't there. He had blown right up in mid-air.'

Lt Warren Shaw was also credited with a single Bf 109 destroyed and Lts Charles Leaf and Hugh Barlow shared credit for a third Messerschmitt, but the two remaining enemy aircraft escaped. One of the downed German pilots was 188-kill *Experte* Hauptmann Joachim Kirschner, commander of IV./JG 27. He successfully bailed out of his stricken aeroplane only to be captured by partisans of the 29th Herzegovinian Striking Division and executed. The 57th pilots then continued their assigned reconnaissance/interdiction mission and located a 75-ft barge and a 200-ft cargo vessel before returning to Amendola at 1615 hrs.

The remainder of December saw a continuous 57th FG presence over the Dalmatian coast, hunting Axis shipping. Additional Thunderbolts were due to be issued to the group in early 1944, but for the remaining December missions P-40s provided the strike element and those available P-47s flew top cover. The group's Thunderbolt pilots saw little action for the rest of the month as a result. On the 19th, while en route to Trogir harbour, eight Bf 109s were sighted at long range but the Thunderbolts were unable to engage them.

Maritime reconnaissance missions on the 18th, 19th and 30th also yielded positive intelligence on Axis shipping in the region, and the 57th's P-40s initiated successful attacks on several vessels, including registering hits on a 6000-ton ship, but winter weather made it increasingly difficult to mount successful operations across the Adriatic. As a result, the group's Thunderbolts would not fire their guns in anger until the second week of January 1944.

Although it has received its theatre identification bands on both wings and tail, 42-75630 has yet to receive its 'number in squadron' fuselage identifier. The 57th's markings standardised on yellow theater ID bands and two-digit side numbers, the latter a carry-over from the group's P-40 days. This particular aeroplane would soon be wearing '52' on the fuselage (*Bob Hanning collection via 57thfightergroup.com/ Mark O'Boyle*)

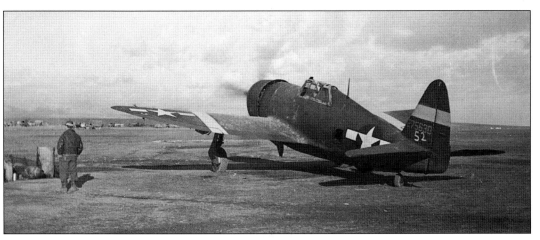

ANTI-SHIPPING AND ANZIO

Terrible weather kept the 57th FG grounded throughout the first week of January, with New Year's Day having been spent salvaging tents and reinforcing stakes after a violent wind and rain storm blew through Amendola. Winds of up to 100 mph destroyed or shredded numerous tents, including the group mess, where the New Year's Day turkey dinner had been prepared. The holiday feast was completely ruined and C-rations were substituted for turkey while the 57th's personnel tried to recover as best they could. The group's spirits lifted somewhat the following day when the storm subsided, living quarters were salvaged and a replacement turkey dinner was finally served.

After a brief respite on the 3rd, foul weather returned, and continued throughout the week before finally clearing on 7 January. Despite better atmospheric conditions, the incessant rain had turned Amendola into an unusable quagmire. British Army engineers worked tirelessly to improve the airfield's drainage, and although a damaged P-38 made an emergency landing on the 7th, Amendola Landing Ground was not declared operational until 10 January.

Group operations began anew the following day when the 64th and 65th FSs were tasked with missions over Yugoslavia. The 'Black Scorpions' of the 64th FS armed each of their P-40s with a single 500-lb bomb and went hunting for Axis shipping. When the unit reached Split harbour, it attacked a 300 ft merchant ship, scoring at least one direct hit. While the 64th pilots were dropping their bombs, the 'Fighting Cocks' of the 65th FS were patrolling over the islands of Vis, Hvar and Brac, at the entrance to Split harbour. The patrol, led by squadron CO Maj Gilbert O Wymond Jr, was relatively uneventful except for some inaccurate, mixed-calibre anti-aircraft fire received from nervous partisan units on Vis. All 12 aeroplanes returned to Amendola safely, however.

The following morning saw the 65th's pilots up early for a 0700 hrs takeoff. The two-hour mission was to be a 12-ship sweep in the same vicinity as the previous day, led by 1Lt Alfred Froning. One Thunderbolt was forced to abort after having mechanical trouble, leaving 11 P-47s to cross the Adriatic and prowl for targets. The unit was at 4000 ft when ten Bf 109s attacked out of the clouds just prior to reaching the coast. A thin overcast at 5000 ft made pursuit a challenge and the enemy chose to stay above the cloud layer, making 'quick darting passes at our "Bolts"'. Capt Richard Hunziker, leading 'Black' section, sighted four of the Bf 109s, called them out and led his flight in pursuit. The first one he engaged took hits, but made it to the safety of the clouds. Hunziker continues;

'I then latched onto the tail of another one and went into a Lufbery with him. I stayed with him for ten turns, but was not able to pull in tight enough to get a shot. I wasn't getting anywhere with him and was losing my speed, so I broke away, my wingman following me. I hit a third from astern and got some good hits, resulting in his aircraft going into a dive and crashing into the side of a mountain.'

Lt Philip Miholich, Hunziker's wingman, stayed with his flight leader and protected his tail during the engagement. A Bf 109 tried to get on Hunziker's tail and Miholich quickly shot him down;

'Our formation pressed the attack in which my flight leader destroyed one Me 109. I saw a second Me 109 on my flight leader's tail and I turned into him, firing a long burst at 90 degrees deflection. I then turned with him and fired a long burst dead astern at a range of 200-300 yards. He then began pouring black smoke and disappeared into the overcast.'

Lts Robert Sherboudy and William Moreau, both still below the cloud layer, confirmed that Miholich's Bf 109 crashed into the sea. Meanwhile, Lt Howard Hickock fired a long burst at a Bf 109 and observed strikes and white smoke pouring from his victim. However, as he pressed the attack, his aeroplane took a number of cannon hits from another Bf 109 and he was forced to break off, nearly losing control of his aeroplane.

1Lt Froning was aggressively going after every Bf 109 he saw, protecting the tails of his squadronmates. '"Ace" Froning was busy giving help all this time, chasing darting MEs off numerous buddies' tails, but evidently those MEs saw the five swastikas on his ship and not wanting to be No 6, made hurriedly toward the cover of clouds, robbing Lt Froning of any good shots', recalled the unit's operations report. Froning did succeed in driving off several Bf 109s that were attacking Lt Burton Andrus's P-47D 42-75712, named *HUN HUNTER II*. However, as the squadron turned to disengage and head home, Andrus suffered a direct flak hit that nearly took his wing off. He was flying Maj Wymond's aeroplane, and despite heavy damage and fire, was able to bring the boss' fighter back to Amendola and land safely.

Lt Hickok's P-47D 42-22804 had also been damaged in the clash, and although he managed to nurse it back across the Adriatic, the aeroplane became uncontrollable just outside of Amendola and he was forced to 'hit the silk' near the airfield. Hickok was quickly picked up by several squadronmates and brought back to the field.

The sobering after effects of a direct hit to the wing root of Gil Wymond's P-47D 42-75712. This aeroplane was flown by Lt Burton Andrus in the dogfight of 12 January 1944. As the flight was turning for home, Andrus' aeroplane was hit and he was forced to coax it back to base (*Bob Hanning collection via 57thfightergroup.com/ Mark O'Boyle*)

Lt Howard Hickok also nursed his wounded P-47 back across the Adriatic on 12 January, but he was forced to bail out when his mount, P-47D 42-22804, became impossible to control (*Bob Hanning collection via 57thfightergroup.com/Mark O'Boyle*)

TRAINING AND MODIFICATION

While the 65th and 66th FSs continued to fly missions in the P-47D and P-40F, respectively, the 64th stood down on 13 January and began an intense training regime to qualify all of its pilots on the Thunderbolt. Over a six-day period all of the squadron's pilots went through transition training, including classes on the P-47's R-2800 powerplant, its armament and how to best utilise the aeroplane's strengths in a fight. Flying the new machine was very different from the P-40, and many pilots who had seen combat in the Warhawk initially did not like the new fighter. The Curtiss

fighter was more agile and could turn inside both the Bf 109 and the P-47. However, the latter's blistering speed in a dive and considerably higher top speed quickly won over its critics. The 64th's transition went smoothly, and a week later the 66th FS stood down from operations and began a similar work-up on the Thunderbolt.

While its sister squadrons prepared to take the P-47 into combat, the 65th FS continued to fly missions over the Yugoslavian coast on 13 and 14 January, but was re-tasked with flying bomber escort missions for the week that followed. The group was assigned a lighter mission load during this time so that it could complete modifications that would allow the Thunderbolt to be used as a dive-bomber.

While underwing racks had been fitted to production Thunderbolts starting with the P-47D-15-RE (Farmingdale) and P-47D-15-RA (Evansville), and had been retrofitted to some earlier blocks, they were designed primarily to drop external fuel tanks. The manual tank release handle was located on the lower left side of the cockpit, making it completely impractical for ordnance delivery. It was nearly impossible for a pilot to enter a dive, maintain his crosshairs on the target and simultaneously release both underwing bombs.

To further compound matters, on early model P-47Ds, the release for the belly bomb rack was located on the right side of the cockpit floor next to the tailwheel lock/unlock lever, making it all but useless for dropping bombs except in straight and level flight. It was moved to the left side of the cockpit and inserted between the other two tank release handles from the P-47D-15 onward, making it difficult, if not impossible for the pilot to pull both wing release handles towards him while in a dive. Maj Gil Wymond tasked MSgt Bill Hahn with creating a field expedient method that would allow pilots to stay focused in their attacks and simultaneously release both wing stores. MSgt Hahn related;

'One could see how awkward it would be to pull the left and right wing release simultaneously. We needed to combine the release handle for the two wing tanks, and this was achieved on the prototype by laying a flat steel bar across the three releases and applying a fulcrum to the floor to enable the pilot – with one pull – to release the wing bombs. This was not a satisfactory application because the belly tank could not be used.'

After some trial and error, Hahn and Sgt Charles Appel devised a system where the release handles were mounted to the floor and, through a cable system, were connected to pull handles on the bottom left side of the instrument panel. This arrangement worked well, but Hahn and Appel continued to refine it, eventually fitting all 57th FG P-47s with a modified version of this system.

With the new release handles installed on all squadron aircraft, Maj Wymond gave the system its first combat test on 23 January. Escorted by five Thunderbolts, he took off with two 1000-lb bombs underwing and attacked the large road bridge over the Krka River near Skradin. While one bomb hit about 50 ft from the end of the bridge, the cloud cover made a steep attack very difficult. Although it was not a very effective dive-bombing demonstration, the

The urgency of combat forced a great deal of innovation. The factory-installed bomb release system in the P-47D was incompatible with dive-bombing operations, so Maj Gil Wymond and MSgt Bill Hahn redesigned it to make ordnance delivery simpler for Thunderbolt pilots. The toggles (two on the left for the wing pylons and a single on the right for the belly rack) are plainly visible on either side of the centre console (*Dwight Orman via Don Kaiser*)

mission proved that the system worked. Later in the day Maj Wymond led the 65th on the first formation P-47 dive-bombing mission. Once again the aircraft headed across the Adriatic, six Thunderbolts (each armed with two 1000-lb bombs) attacking the Krka River bridge for a second time. The remaining four aeroplanes in the formation provided top cover.

Repaired and ready to fly again, Maj Gil Wymond taxis *Hun Hunter II* out on another combat mission in February 1944 (*Bob Hanning collection via 57thfighter group.com/Mark O'Boyle*)

A 5000 ft ceiling prevented the 'Thunderbombers' from initiating steep dives on the target, forcing them to commence their attacks from just 1500 ft. Accuracy was somewhat less than intended as a result. One bomb struck the bridge on the northern end of the span, while the remainder fell on the southern approach, causing massive cratering on the road. While the desired effect of this new capability was not fully realised, the mission was an overall success, and ushered in a new phase for the Thunderbolt in the air-to-ground role.

Despite the moderate success of the first trial missions, dive-bombing was standardised as a group mission, and the 64th was quickly brought up to speed on the proper techniques for performing such attacks in the P-47. Modification of all 57th FG aeroplanes took some time, and the 65th remained the primary dive-bombing unit through to mid-February.

Escort missions, however, were still part of the 57th's repertoire, and on 29 January the 65th was ordered to delouse a returning formation of B-25s from the 12th, 321st and 340th BGs. Climbing to 13,000 ft at their assigned rendezvous point, the fighters failed to locate the Mitchells. The flight of eight P-47s continued to patrol in the Foligno-Perugia area in the hope of picking up the bomber formation. Instead of B-25s, the flight sighted a formation of ten Bf 109s ten miles north of Perugia, headed south at 18,000 ft. Dropping their belly tanks, the formation climbed to engage the Messerschmitts. Lt Burton Andrus fired first, putting several hundred rounds of 0.50-cal ammunition into the nearest Bf 109 and causing it to pour white smoke, roll over on its back and

Maj Gil Wymond and three members of the 57th FG pose with one of the Headquarters flight Thunderbolts (*Author's collection*)

crash. No other claims were made against the formation and the P-47s broke contact quickly, with one of their number damaged, but flyable, and returned to Amendola.

January 1944 closed with two of the 57th's three units completely converted to the P-47 and the third's conversion well underway. The group finished out the month with a big anti-shipping day for both the 64th and 65th FSs. Since not all of its aeroplanes were yet modified with the new bomb release system, the 64th FS was sent on a strafing mission to Trogir harbour across the Adriatic. Nine P-47s found a camouflaged 150 ft motor torpedo boat and made numerous

Targets in Yugoslavia usually consisted of trains, motor transport and anything that might be of use to the Axis. Targets of opportunity were plentiful in German-controlled Yugoslavia and anything that moved was fair game for P-47s out on long-range fighter sweeps (*USAF World War 2 Collection*)

passes on it, leaving the vessel burning. A P-47 in the formation also sighted and strafed a 75 ft three-masted schooner.

The 64th returned to Amendola at 1055 hrs, and 30 minutes later, a formation of 11 65th aeroplanes was headed back to Rogoznica harbour to interdict a concentration of small surface craft. Diving down from 6000 ft, the P-47 pilots strafed the boats with devastating effect, leaving a number burning. 1Lt Philip Miholich, leading the second element of the lead flight in P-47D 42-75637, took several hits in the engine from small arms fire. His wingman, 1Lt Donald Harward followed him down;

'I was about 150 yards behind Miholich in the dive. He was smoking slightly as he pulled up from the target. He pulled up to about 2500 ft, and by then black smoke was coming from the belly of his ship. His nose dropped and he lost about 500 ft before he bailed out. He dropped in the water about 200 yards off shore, two miles south of the target.'

Miholich was then seen to inflate his 'Mae West' life vest as the rest of the flight circled overhead until they were at critically low fuel levels and were forced to return to base. At Amendola, the 64th received word of a downed aviator and launched a four-aircraft search mission at 1420 hrs. The P-47s reached Rogoznica and patrolled over Lt Miholich's last known position. Although green colouring from Miholich's dye marker was still visible in the water, he was not seen and the search was called off. Unknown to his squadronmates, he had been picked up by fishermen and brought to the partisan HQ in Trogir, where he remained for several months before being smuggled back to Italy via the Partisan underground on the island of Vis. Miholich returned to the 57th and flew a few more combat missions, but was sent home when the group moved to Corsica.

Poor weather continued through February and hampered operations on a regular basis. The 66th FS completed its transition to the Thunderbolt and flew its first mission – escorting B-25s of the 321st BG on an attack on Viterbo – on 3 February. Cloud cover prevented the bombers from hitting their target and no contact was made with several unidentified fighters that were seen some distance from the B-25s.

Weather continued to have a negative effect on operations throughout the week, and it was not until 8 February that the first significant combat sorties of the month were flown. The 66th scored its first P-47 motor transport kills during a strafing mission along the Popoli-Avezzano-Sora road. Tasked with attacking a vehicle convoy, the only targets sighted by pilots from the unit were two trucks that were strafed and left burning. Later that day, a flight of 12 66th aeroplanes again escorted B-25s of the 321st BG to their target. This time, despite cloud, the bombers dropped their loads on Orta with only minimal heavy-calibre flak opposition.

The 64th FS flew one of its more obscure missions of the war on 23 February when the squadron was tasked with escorting Operation *Manhole* – a flight of glider-towing C-47s of the 51st Troop Carrier Wing carrying a high level British and Soviet delegation to meet with Yugoslavian partisans. 'Black Scorpions'' pilots rendezvoused with their charges over Termiti Island at 5000 ft at 1100 hrs and the formation climbed to 15,000 ft. Cloud cover over the target was almost total, but two of the three C-47s got below it and released their gliders.

Operating at the extreme end of their combat radius, three P-47s were forced to turn back shortly after reaching the target area and land at the airfield occupied by the RAF's No 239 Wing. The remainder of the flight returned to Amendola on fumes after a three-and-a-half-hour flight.

The 57th FG ended February with a roar, sending 24 aircraft on an interdiction mission to Dubrovnik. Twelve P-47s from the 66th, led by Capts Charles Leaf and William Benedict, were the strike element, armed with two 500-lb bombs each, while the other 12 from the 65th provided top cover for the attackers. Their primary target was a 6000-ton vessel in the harbour and any additional shipping in the area.

Reaching Dubrovnik harbour at 3000 ft under a 5000 ft overcast ceiling, the 57th's Thunderbolts sighted a pair of 200-ft vessels at anchor. Capt Leaf led the formation down and put his bombs directly amidships one of the vessels, leaving it burning. Once their bombs were expended on the ships, the flight made several strafing attacks on nearby barracks buildings on the island at the harbour's entrance, destroying them. Two aircraft flown by Capt Benedict and Lt Wise then separated from the flight to reconnoitre the coastline south from Dubrovnik. They located and strafed two stationary trains, one southbound and one northbound, that appeared to be transferring supplies. Their attack resulted in a large secondary explosion, cutting the rail line and destroying both trains.

Benedict and Wise continued their two-man wrecking crew as they headed south and strafed a tug towing a barge with a crane on it, damaging the latter and leaving the former listing heavily as they pulled away. The pilots rejoined the formation and the group turned for Amendola. All 12 P-47s from the 66th were accounted for as they headed back across the Adriatic. Flt Off Stern's aeroplane had suffered some damage in the initial shipping attack, but it remained with the flight and returned without incident.

The 66th FS finally became operational with the Thunderbolt in February 1944. Here, newly arrived 42-75678 (an early Block 15 aeroplane) undergoes a maintenance run-up. Other than the number-in-squadron identifier, no identifying markings had been added at this point, which would date this photograph as having been taken between late December 1943 and mid March 1944 (*Author's Collection*)

MORE THUNDERBOLTS IN-THEATRE

While the 57th ramped up to full group-level Thunderbolt operations on the eastern coast of Italy, the Allied amphibious assault on Anzio had come to a stalemate. Operation *Shingle's* initial landings at Anzio on 22 January were relatively unopposed, and units like the 6615th Ranger Force (provisional), 3rd Infantry Division and 509th Parachute Infantry Battalion seized their D-Day objectives with little resistance. However, instead of striking inland, VI Corps' operational commander, Maj Gen John P Lucas, chose to consolidate his gains and wait for resupply. This inaction allowed German forces under Generalfeldmarschall Albert Kesselring to reinforce their positions and surround the invaders, resulting in a near World War 1-style stalemate by the end of the month.

A great deal of air power within the theatre was redirected to assist the invasion force, and as winter turned into spring, several units were moved to better support the beachhead. The 79th FG moved to Capodichino airfield, outside of Naples, in January and provided a significant number of close support sorties over the beachhead. Its Warhawks had performed admirably in the fighter-bomber role since late 1942, but it was clear that these war-weary mounts needed replacing with a new aeroplane that could carry a greater payload farther and faster.

The 79th's first P-47s arrived at Capodichino on 8 February, with each squadron allocated three airframes for transition training. As more arrived in-theatre, and the Fifteenth Air Force's 325th FG gave up its Thunderbolts in favour of the P-51 for long-range escort work, the Twelfth's two designated P-47 groups received new airframes to replace combat losses for the 57th and to bring the 79th up to full strength.

The latter group's 86th FS completed its transition training and was certified to begin combat operations by the first week of March. While uneventful, the group's first combat mission, flown on 9 March, was an eight-aircraft patrol over the Anzio beachhead at 15,000 ft looking for German fighters. The day was marred, however, by Flt Off Vincent Wall's crash in former 64th FS aeroplane P-47D 42-22810 on a fuel consumption test flight near Venosa airfield. Wall was declared missing after he failed to return, but confirmation of his death would not reach the squadron for another two days. The circumstances of his crash were never determined. Wall was an accomplished aviator with more than 1100 hours of flight time, having been with the squadron since North Africa.

The following day, Capt George W Ewing Jr took command of the 86th from Maj Melvin Nielsen, who was moved up to become the group's deputy commander. Ewing had also flown P-40s with the squadron in North Africa, and was a well respected member of the 'Comanche' squadron.

Movement to a new airfield usually happened as a two-phase operation, with the air and ground elements arriving separately. Here, the groundcrews of the 86th FS have just arrived at Capodichino and are hauling out their tents to establish a new bivouac area (*USAF World War 2 Collection*)

The 85th FS repeated the 86th's misfortune on the 11th when it flew a similar profile eight-aircraft mission, with no enemy contact, to commence the P-47 phase of its MTO operations. That morning, 2Lt Raymond Higgins took off on a local transition flight in the Capodichino area, and he was last seen by his flight at 30,000 ft entering a near vertical dive. Higgins' aircraft had almost certainly suffered an oxygen system failure, causing the pilot to black out. Had he awoken at a lower altitude, pulling out of the dive would have been nearly impossible for compressibility would have rendered the P-47 uncontrollable as its airspeed increased in the dive. As the aeroplane approached the speed of sound, the shockwave coming off its nose would blank out control authority on the elevator surfaces, making it impossible to pull out of the high speed dive. P-47D 42-74956 hit the ground at an extremely high rate of speed, leaving a crater nearly 20 ft deep and 30 ft wide.

March's routine fighter sweeps yielded minimal results through to the 13th, but they proved an incremental and effective combat introduction for the 79th FG's Thunderbolts. In a break from this routine, on the 11th a flight of seven Thunderbolts from the 86th FS were vectored by local ground controller 'Grubsteak' to locate and provide cover for a downed aircrew in the water 30 miles off the Anzio coast. Four dinghies were located and the flight remained on station, circling the airmen until the Air-Sea Rescue boat was within five miles and a flight of RAF Spitfires had arrived on-scene to relieve them.

MOVEMENT

As the 79th began flying combat patrols over the Anzio beachhead, additional fighter units were being reassigned to airfields closer to Anzio in order to support the bogged down VI Corps. The 57th was ordered west to Cercola, where it shared the small field with the 324th FG. The two groups had worked closely in North Africa, and for the 57th it was a doubly sweet homecoming as the unit was now back under American operational control and again working alongside the 324th.

The 66th FS quickly acclimated to its new surroundings, and on 14 March the squadron was ordered to dive bomb the railway station at Fara Sabina. Armed with two 500-lb bombs apiece and diving from 3000 ft, the 'Exterminators'' P-47s scored direct hits on the station and surrounding marshalling yards, starting fires that resulted in a large column of black smoke. As the lead element pulled up from their bomb run, three Fw 190s were sighted and the P-47s gave chase.

Surprisingly, the German formation split up, two Fw 190s of I./JG 2 diving under the Thunderbolts and the third climbing away from them. Lt Donald Bell dove to follow the two and quickly latched onto the tail of one of the fighters. Closing to within 250 yards, he opened fire, seeing strikes all along the fuselage and wing roots. The Focke-Wulf pilot bailed out of his fighter and Lt Robert Schuren, who was flying as Bell's wingman, was able to confirm the victory when he saw the pilotless aeroplane crash.

Meanwhile, Lt Walter Henson went after the other Fw 190, firing several bursts and seeing numerous hits on the enemy aircraft, before breaking off his attack. He lost sight of the stricken Fw 190, but Capt Thomas Liston was able to confirm the victory when he saw the fighter go straight into the ground. The third Focke-Wulf that had chosen to climb above the P-47s escaped without harm.

The 85th and 86th FSs launched an 18-aircraft bomber escort/fighter sweep on the morning of St Patrick's Day. Although two aeroplanes developed mechanical trouble and had to turn back, the remaining 16 escorted B-25s of the 340th BG in to the target at Rocasecca and back to the bomb line. Once the bombers were safely over friendly territory, the formation broke away and headed out on a fighter sweep over the beachhead. They quickly sighted a formation of roughly 20 Fw 190s, with a top cover of ten Bf 109s diving down from 15,000 ft to attack targets on the ground. The flight intercepted the Messerschmitts at 12,000 ft and a five-minute fight ensued. Pilots of the 85th were the first to engage, with Capt Carl Stewart leading his flight into the fray and immediately getting onto the tail of a diving Bf 109. 'Closing in, firing dead astern, the ME began smoking. At 2000 ft the German aircraft half-rolled and plunged into the ground'.

Meanwhile, Lt Charles DeFoor, also in Stewart's flight, got on the tail of another Bf 109 and expended nearly every one of the 2100 0.50-cal rounds that his aeroplane carried on the diving Messerschmitt. In the face of such a heavy volume of fire the enemy aeroplane burst into flames and never pulled out of its dive.

Lt Maxwell, diving with the rest of the formation, also engaged a single Bf 109 and fired several bursts at it, seeing hits, but he was then forced to disengage when he blacked out while recovering from his dive. In their first air-to-air engagement with the Thunderbolt, 85th FS pilots were credited with two Bf 109s destroyed and one damaged. Although Capts Risden Wall and Martin chased several more Messerschmitts from the same formation to the outskirts of Rome, the 86th would have to wait until May to chalk up its first aerial victories with the P-47.

Closer to home, Mount Vesuvius had rumbled for the better part of early March, and on the 18th it erupted in a massive cloud of ash and created miles-long lava flows that destroyed several small Italian villages in their path. The hot ash thrown into the air had the potential to damage aircraft, burn fabric-covered control surfaces and melt Plexiglas. The 57th and 324th FGs at nearby Cercola were ordered to evacuate immediately to airfields outside the path of the ash cloud. While the 324th settled in at the 79th's base at Capodichino, the 57th moved to Corsica, where it was established as a separate air task force to take the lead in upcoming operations.

P-47s from the 57th FG are hurriedly prepared at Cercola for the group's move to Corsica following the eruption of Mount Vesuvius on 19 March 1944. This natural disaster caused havoc in southern Italy, with airfields in the path of the ash cloud being evacuated as quickly as possible. Nevertheless, a number of B-25s and P-40s were badly damaged by the volcanic ash (*Author's collection*)

OPERATION *STRANGLE*

Over the previous months, the Thunderbolt had been proven as an effective ground attack aeroplane. Its hard-hitting main battery of eight 0.50-cal machine guns had a force of impact akin to that of a bus hitting an object at high speed, and with new modifications it had become a devastating dive-bomber as well. Allied air planners realised the effectiveness of this aeroplane and created a key role in the new air campaign that would fully exploit the P-47's strengths.

Allied Forces HQ, still based in Tunisia under the command of Field Marshal Sir Henry Maitland Wilson, believed that the stalemate on the Anzio beachhead could be broken by starving out the Wehrmacht and forcing it to retreat so as to shorten its supply lines. As the name implied, the purpose of Operation *Strangle* was to choke off German logistics through air interdiction, forcing a retreat from the beachhead. Utilising lessons learned from the campaign against the island of Pantelleria as evidence of air power's ability to shape the ground battle and make the enemy surrender simply by air attack, the Mediterranean Allied Air Force (MAAF) believed that it was possible to force a German withdrawal from the 'Gustav Line' through attacks on the enemy's supply network.

The principle method of transportation and supply delivery for German forces in Italy was the country's extensive rail network that stretched from the Austrian border down to the southern tip of the Italian 'boot'. The order to execute *Strangle* was issued on 19 March 1944, and it prioritised the Italian rail system as the No 1 target. The Mediterranean Allied Strategic Air Force (MASAF, which included the B-17 and B-24 units of the Fifteenth Air Force) was tasked with destroying marshalling yards in northern Italy, while MATAF (comprised of the Tactical Twelfth Air Force and the RAF's DAF) medium bombers were then tasked with destroying infrastructure within a belt across the country north of Rome

An all too common sight during the rainy Italian spring of 1944. Cercola airfield was flooded for a number of days during March of that year, preventing missions from being flown (*USAF World War 2 Collection*)

between Siena and Genoa on the west coast, and from Ancona north to Rimini on the east coast.

South of this 'interdiction belt', XII Air Support Command (ASC) fighter-bombers were free to roam, cutting rail lines and junctions and destroying trains and any other means used to transport supplies to frontline German units.

Orders for this new operation quickly filtered down through XII ASC, and the 57th and 79th FGs began focusing their efforts on railway bridges. Its dive-bombing capability made the P-47 the weapon of choice when attacking the multitude of smaller bridges that dotted the Italian countryside. The Twelfth's medium bomber forces went after the larger bridges while XII ASC's P-47s, P-40s and A-36s laid waste any remaining spans. Since the P-47 could carry more than twice the bomb load of the other two types, the 'Thunderbombers' of the 57th FG were kept busy throughout March as they geared up for the move to Corsica.

Meanwhile, the latter half of March saw a sharp increase in bomber escort missions for the 79th FG as a result of *Strangle*. Prior to the 20th, the 79th had flown just five escort missions for the that month. After *Strangle* came into effect, it performed an additional 13 in the last ten days of the month. Since only one of the group's P-47s had been fitted with the proper modifications for dive-bombing, the 79th was tasked with protecting Twelfth Air Force medium bombers targeting railway bridges, marshalling yards and major junctions within the interdiction belt.

However, as a taste of things to come, on 23 March the 85th FS CO, Maj John Martin had his P-47 (the lone bomb rack-equipped aeroplane in the group) loaded with two 1000-lb GP bombs for a combat test of the Thunderbolt's dive-bombing capability. Escorted by Capt Carl Stewart, Martin headed for Gaeta Point to destroy a gun emplacement that had been harassing Allied shipping, but overcast skies prevented him from demonstrating the P-47's impressive dive-bombing capability. Turning for home, he jettisoned both bombs over the Tyrrhenian Sea.

The following day, the 85th FS returned to escort duties when 12 Thunderbolts headed to the Orvieto railway bridge with B-26s of the 320th BG. As the Marauders began their bomb run, Bf 109s of 8./JG 53 bounced the escorts out of the sun. The twelve Messerschmitts split into two sections of six, each attacking one of two four-ship P-47 sections. 1Lt Powell Schuemack, leading 'Yellow' section at 14,000 ft, called out a warning to 'Red' section before the Bf 109s struck, but almost simultaneously the second group of German fighters attacked his section. Prior to engaging the Bf 109s attacking him, Schuemack recalled seeing the No 2 aeroplane in 'Red' section going down trailing thick black smoke. He was then quickly drawn into the fight around him.

1Lt Albert Benz, leading 'Red' flight, saw the incoming Bf 109s as Schuemack's warning came over the radio. He quickly sighted the Messerschmitts attacking from 'seven o'clock high' and turned his flight into them. The Germans had set up a perfect ambush, and as the P-47s turned toward their attackers, four more hit them from behind, focusing their attention on Lt Ward Pringle's Thunderbolt, P-47D 42-22853. His aeroplane was last seen in a dive, billowing black smoke, with two Bf 109s on his tail. While no one saw him crash, no parachute was seen and Lt Pringle was officially listed as Missing In Action.

The 57th FG began its contribution to *Strangle* on the 24th with a 64th FS eight-aircraft armed railway reconnaissance mission between Civitavecchia and Capranica. The 'Black Scorpions' flew up the coastline and made landfall at Civitavecchia, before turning northeast to begin their reconnoitring. Their primary target was a three-span, concrete rail bridge northeast of Civitavecchia, which was easily located. All eight aeroplanes initiated their dives at 3000 ft and placed their 500-lb bombs on the bridge's western approach, scoring numerous hits and successfully cutting the railway lines on all three spans. According to 1Lt Paul Carll;

'Our flight formed up after the run and we did a turnabout to come home. It was at this point that we were attacked by 10+ enemy aircraft.'

The flight quickly turned to engage the formation of ten yellow-nosed Fw 190s from I./JG 2, as Carll recalled;

'The enemy made a split attack, with two ships coming in on Lt Loyst Towners' tail and three on my tail. Our element did a turnabout into the enemy and the last time I saw Towners there were two ships on his tail and he didn't appear to be making an attempt to shake them.'

Once the flight turned into their attackers, the fight was on. Lt Michael McCarthy, a veteran pilot who had been with the 64th FS since Sicily, described the engagement;

'These guys were aggressive, flew excellent formation, climbed quickly to attack out of the sun, maintained two-ship integrity and avoided the turning dogfight unless they had the advantage. I remember turning with one on the opposite side of the tight circle in a 90-degree bank, neither of us gaining on the other. I saw gun flashes from his aeroplane, thought to myself "No way", but he actually put three shells into my P-47, one in front of the windshield and two more behind the cockpit. That is the lowest percentage shot in a dogfight, requiring the maximum lead and a full 90-degree deflection. I was impressed.'

However, McCarthy's friend Lt Bill Nuding was an equally good shot and caught another Focke-Wulf with a 90-degree deflection shot, knocking pieces off the aeroplane and sending it out of control. He followed it down, but was engaged by another Fw 190 and was unable to confirm the first fighter's demise. While Lt Bruce Abercrombie was chasing another Fw 190 that he scored several hits on, he saw a smoking fighter crash into the ground out of control, confirming Nuding's kill. In the meantime, Abercrombie's quarry began to billow white smoke and its pilot struggled to maintain control. After another burst from Abercrombie's eight 0.50-cal guns, his target appeared to spin out of control, but the skilled pilot in the Fw 190 was able to keep flying and escape, leaving Abercrombie with credit for a damaged Focke-Wulf.

While the 64th was engaged with elements of JG 2, a formation of nine 66th FS Thunderbolts was working over a ten-wagon train. Initial bombing results were less than spectacular, but the formation strafed on its second pass, destroying the locomotive and damaging several wagons. Another 15 wagons were found in a siding close by and were strafed and left burning. En route back to Caserta, the formation intercepted a solitary Bf 109, which Lt Donald Smith shot down in flames. The day ended on a sad note, however, when a flight of RAF Spitfires attacked 66th FS Thunderbolts on their second mission of the day. The P-47s were at 12,000 ft over the Tyrrhenian Sea when the Spitfires attacked. 2Lt Leon Jansen was in the low flight and saw the entire engagement;

'When we were just west of the Anzio beachhead three bogies were called in at a position of "three o'clock" to our formation. As we proceeded north, I watched the three bogies going south. They turned ten degrees and began overtaking us. The flight of four aeroplanes that were giving us top cover were also flying at 12,000 ft, slightly to our right. The bogies were closing in on our top cover, and when they were within about 350 yards range I easily identified them as Spitfire VIIIs.

'One Spit closed right on in to a range of about 100-150 yards and fired a short burst at Lt Coughlin, who was flying on Lt McCoy's wing. Coughlin pulled up in sort of a wing-over and began a split-S. The Spitfire followed him through this manoeuvre. Coughlin's aeroplane was smoking badly when he started down. He went straight down, hitting the water half-a-mile from shore. I watched him from the time the Spit began firing until he hit the water. When his P-47 struck the water it exploded, and flame was seen at that point for about two or three minutes.'

The 57th FG finished March at a run, each squadron flying two or three missions a day against railway infrastructure south of the interdiction belt. The Luftwaffe only came up to challenge the 64th FS on the afternoon of 29 March, and Maj Art Exon caught a Bf 109 from a flight of four at 5000 ft, and it blew up after a concentrated burst from his guns. Lt John J Lenihan quickly latched onto another Messerschmitt and saw pieces fly off the fighter and smoke billow from its engine, but the aircraft escaped into the clouds before he could deliver a killing burst. A week later Lenihan would have another opportunity to claim a kill.

The 79th FG continued to fly escort missions through to month-end. On 30 March it returned to Orvieto with 24 B-25s of the 321st BG. Crossing the coastline near Civitavecchia, the formation was almost immediately attacked by a flight of 12 Fw 190s, but the Thunderbolts of the 85th and 86th FSs successfully kept them away from the bomber force. To exploit the B-25's lightly defended underbelly, the Fw 190s dove from 12,000 ft and then zoom-climbed up underneath the bombers cruising at 11,000 ft. However, the escorts were ready. Capt Stewart led the intercept, catching a Focke-Wulf from dead astern and setting its right wing on fire. The Fw 190 tried to manoeuvre but its wing separated from the fuselage and the fighter spiralled into the ground.

Lt Pierre Guachon, a Free French pilot assigned to the 79th FG to train on the P-47, dove on four Focke-Wulfs as they climbed to attack the bombers, firing several short bursts at one from less than 100 yards astern. His intended victim began to trail black smoke and half-rolled over into a steep dive. Not wasting time, he climbed back to altitude and

Since the majority of German supplies to its 10th and 14th Armies arrived in Italy by rail, the key aim of *Strangle* was the destruction of the Italian rail network (*USAF*)

engaged the first elements of another enemy formation of Bf 109s from either JG 27, JG 53 or JG 77. Guachon came in head-on at one of the fighters, forcing the pilot to break away. He then dove onto the Bf 109's tail, firing several bursts and seeing strikes on its fuselage, but the Messerschmitt reached cloud cover and escaped. He was credited with a probable Fw 190 and a damaged Bf 109.

Two P-47s were lost as a result of the engagement. Lt Milo Klear turned his stricken aeroplane for home after being hit by several cannon shells, but he was forced to bail out over friendly territory and was back at Capodichino by nightfall. 1Lt Schuemack was wounded when a cannon shell exploded by his cockpit, spraying his leg with shrapnel and knocking out his radio. He was able to nurse his stricken aeroplane back to friendly territory, but with a rough-running engine and few remaining options, Schuemack chose to bail out. He landed safely among British troops, who tended his wounds prior to returning him to Capodichino.

But the mission was not over yet. As the bombers completed their runs and turned for home, Capt Edward Byron (the Group Operations Officer) sighted a lone 'Messerschmitt' – possibly an Arado Ar 96 trainer – and dove to attack it. 'He fired at a very close range and the ME slow rolled and its engine burst into flame. He gave it three more long bursts and the aircraft fell through the overcast out of control at 9000 ft'.

Byron sighted a second Messerschmitt as the bombers approached the western Italian coast and closed to within 100 yards before opening fire. 'He fired four bursts from dead astern, shooting away a very large section of the Hun's aircraft, and smoke was seen coming from the engine. The ME spun through the overcast in the vicinity of Viterbo'. Byron was credited with one confirmed and one probably destroyed.

By now the cloud cover had become a solid overcast, which made it nearly impossible for the Thunderbolts to return to Capodichino. One managed to land safely, but the remainder of the flight was diverted to other airfields. The majority landed at Taranto, with one at Pomigliano. Lt Guachon bellied his P-47 near Benevento, escaping injury, while Lt Malin Eltzroth straggled in at 1700 hrs and landed safely at Capodichino.

It is of particular interest to note that the 79th FG kill claims of 30 March are detailed in the unit's mission reports, intelligence summaries and daily journals, but whether due to oversight or delays caused by the confusion that ensued as the 85th's pilots attempted to return to base through the solid overcast, the squadron's claims for this date are not listed in the official USAAF Aerial Victories record.

April saw the 79th FG come fully into the fighter-bomber business when the 86th FS became the first unit to be outfitted with newer bomb rack-equipped Block 15 P-47Ds. It flew its first fighter-bomber mission on 2 April, CO Maj Melvin Nielsen leading the dive-bombing attack on a key road junction in support of *Strangle*. Eight P-47s initiated their attacks from 2500 ft and 16 500-lb bombs struck in a loose pattern around the target area. A second dive-bombing mission was flown that afternoon, led by Lt John McNeal. Again, a critical road junction was targeted with a similar number of bombs, this time with better accuracy.

The 86th continued to fly similar operations during the first week of April, while the 85th primarily provided fighter escort for *Strangle* medium bomber missions. New aeroplanes were reaching the group at an

A flaming Ar 96 caught by a P-47 gun camera, quite possibly that fitted to the aircraft of Capt Ed Byron, who claimed a lone 'Me 109' on 30 March that went up in flames. The Messerschmitt fighter and the Arado trainer shared a similar planform (*USAF World War 2 Collection*)

increasing rate by this point, and the 85th flew its first bombing mission on the afternoon of 11 April. Its fourth scheduled operation of the day was an eight-ship dive-bombing mission to Gaeta. Despite large-calibre and very accurate flak, the Thunderbolt pilots scored direct hits in the centre of the town with six of the eight 1000-lb GP bombs dropped.

Four days later, the 86th set a new record. While the P-47 had proven it could carry a 2500-lb load during testing, it had never been attempted on a combat mission. At 1500 hrs on 15 April, three 'Comanche' Thunderbolts took off from Capodichino, each carrying two 1000-lb bombs under the wings and a single 500-lb weapon on the centreline rack, bound for Cassino. The P-47s dove from 3000 ft, and although two 1000-lb bombs failed to release, those that were dropped found their marks and proved that the aircraft could haul more than twice the bomb load of its predecessors, deliver them more accurately in close proximity to friendly forces and retain the capability to fight their way back home.

The morning of 18 April called for an early launch for a 12-ship dive-bombing mission against the railway bridge at Faleri. At 0805 hrs Lt Saverio Martino, leading the formation, sighted the bridge and railway line from 13,000 ft and led the flight down. Light flak was intense and accurate as the P-47s came over the target area. As the fighter-bombers split up and then commenced their diving attacks, a large formation of Fw 190s attempted to intercept them. Capt Wall was leading 'Blue' section, and he pulled up off the target to the left after dropping his bombs in order to see the remainder of his section's bomb run;

'The last aircraft of my flight was piloted by 2Lt Don N Mulkey, and as he released his bombs and started to pull up, his P-47 received direct hits of light, very intense ground fire and small arms fire. I saw him start to climb with flames coming from beneath the belly of his aircraft. He got to 4500 ft and rolled over onto his back and his ship went in, flaming all the way to the ground, where it disintegrated.'

Although hit repeatedly in his dive, Lt Mulkey scored direct hits on the bridge span with his 500-lb bombs.

Once the Thunderbolts had dropped their bombs and turned to engage the Focke-Wulf formation, only eight enemy aircraft remained in the vicinity. Of those eight, six headed north and left the area while two chose to engage the P-47s. Capt Wall fired on the first Focke-Wulf, but broke off his attack when the second got on his tail. Turning into his attacker, he quickly got onto the fighter's tail and despatched his foe with several bursts from his 0.50-cal machine guns. He followed the Fw 190 down and observed the crash. Lts William West and Ray Hagler engaged the first Focke-Wulf and destroyed it, sharing credit for the kill.

TRANSITIONS OLD AND NEW

The 87th FS had held onto its P-40F/Ls, performing dedicated fighter-bomber missions during March and April while the remainder of the group converted to the Thunderbolt. Without its dedication, flying war-weary aeroplanes in an increasingly dangerous role, the 79th FG would have left a significant gap in air cover over the Anzio beachhead. The 87th finally received its first ten P-47s on 18 April, with ten more arriving the next day, but it continued flying the P-40 until the 22nd. Since the 'Skeeters'' pilots had already been checked out in the Thunderbolt, they flew their first mission in their new mounts on the 23rd, hitting the marshalling yards at Orte, after a year of combat in the P-40.

Two P-47s broke off from the main flight and dropped a pair of 500-lb bombs on the harbour at Gaeta Point while inbound to the primary target. The remainder attacked the marshalling yards and surrounding facilities, putting 19 500-lb bombs in the target area and scoring direct hits on four warehouses and storage sheds, causing massive explosions and cutting the rail lines in at least two places. A second mission flown at 1800 hrs only reinforced the fact that the 87th was deadly accurate in its new aeroplanes, and would contribute significantly to *Strangle*.

One of the more unusual targets that the 87th encountered came in the early morning hours of 30 April when 14 aeroplanes located a German radar station with a large rotating aerial and several camouflaged buildings. The formation had already bombed a cluster of ten German vehicles, destroying three and damaging the rest. The radar station was identified as the flight pulled up from their initial dive, and after several strafing passes the aerial and associated buildings were left burning.

As the 87th received new fighters and began flying combat missions, another veteran unit started turning in its war-weary airframes for P-47s. The 27th FG had arrived in North African in late 1942 and had established an impressive record with the A-36. By early 1944, however, with spare parts stocks dwindling and no new Apaches coming off the production line, it was clear that the two A-36-equipped groups (27th and 86th), would need to consolidate so as to keep their aeroplanes flying. The 27th duly handed over its A-36s in February 1944 and used war-weary P-40F/Ls until an adequate number of P-47s were available.

As with most fighter groups in the Mediterranean, rumours of what new type of aeroplane the 27th FG would receive ran rampant. Many hoped for the pure fighter version of their beloved A-36, but considering the mission they had performed so well, most expected to transition to the P-47. The first indication that the group was to receive Thunderbolts was the sudden infusion of replacement pilots all trained on the Republic fighter, and by April the 524th FS had received a few P-47s for transition purposes. These were war-weary D-models without bomb racks that had been cast off from the 57th and 79th, and they were relegated to training duties until the squadron received its complement of aircraft. Lt Sayre had the 524th's first mishap on 12 April when he was forced to belly land his mount due to a runaway prop. Six days later, the majority of the 524th's pilots boarded a C-47 bound for Algiers in order to ferry back brand new P-47s to the squadron's Castel Volturno base.

The unit's daily journal recalled on 24 April, 'There are 27 P-47s assigned to our Squadron. Our Crew Chiefs are practically working double time maintaining both the P-40s and P-47s. Pilots are getting at least 15 hours of transition flying before any attempt will be made to fly any combat missions in the P-47's'. Like the 57th and 79th before it, the 524th quickly realised the strain placed on groundcrews and pilots without a significant stand down to transition to a new airframe.

CORSICA

While the 79th resumed full-scale fighter-bomber operations and the 27th began the transition process, the 57th was moved to Alto airfield on the island of Corsica. Moving the group to this strategic location placed a much larger area of enemy territory within operational radius. Not only was the 57th targeting Axis forces on the Italian mainland, but it was now able to hit key targets in southern France too.

The move also designated the 57th FG as a separate task force that had been specially created to interdict the Italian railway infrastructure. The group's effectiveness and innovation in adapting the P-47 to the fighter-bomber role had placed it in high demand for tactical interdiction missions, and designating it a separate task force eliminated the potential for retasking the group's squadrons for escort or patrol work.

Both the 'Black Scorpions' and 'Fighting Cocks' flew their first missions from Corsica on 1 April, while the 'Exterminators' flew from Cercola, on the mainland. All three squadrons launched 16 aeroplanes to hit different railway bridges and rolling stock in western Italy. XII ASC had ordered the 57th to generate 48 fighter-bomber sorties per day while on Corsica, and the group's first day of combat from the island had seen it meet that challenge thanks to all three squadrons flying a single mission on the 1st. Within 48 hours the squadrons were averaging two missions per day, thus exceeding all expectations.

On the afternoon of 6 April four 'Black Scorpions' P-47s took off from Alto to reconnoitre the railway lines from Lake Trasimeno to Florence. Their objective was to identify potential dive-bombing targets and to engage any targets of opportunity that arose. Two trains were quickly strafed, setting one locomotive ablaze and damaging six wagons as the fast moving flight headed down the line. A number of damaged but serviceable bridges were seen and several pristine bridges and tunnels were noted for future reference. As the flight of four came to the end of their route reconnaissance six miles south of Florence and climbed to altitude, they sighted a flight of 11 Italian bombers down on the deck. Quickly identifying them as ten obsolete BR.20Ms and a single SM.79, the flight dove to attack. The Italians immediately split their formation in two to evade the diving P-47s. Capt Louis Frank led the charge;

'We saw the formation below us and quickly positioned ourselves for an attack. The bombers split into two sections – I went after one section, with my wingman following. As one of the bombers came into my sights, I pushed the button and saw tracers hit the left engine and fuselage. The aeroplane caught fire and spun into the deck. It couldn't have been more than ten seconds later that another bomber made the mistake of getting into my gunsight, and with only a short burst, he was on fire and spinning in. My wingman saw him hit the ground and explode.

'I saw another bomber a short distance away. I fired on him and saw hits on the fuselage, and my wingman, Lt R K Nevett, also got some target practice. His guns were true, with strikes near the cockpit, but this one was a little tougher. Our aeroplanes were faster and overshot him, and by the time we were able to turn about he had disappeared.'

When the flight landed, it was discovered that Lt Nevett's aeroplane was the only one of the three that had been hit by any return fire.

Maj Carlton Chamberlain, leading the second element, also engaged the bombers, quickly 'splashing' a BR.20M;

'I saw Capt Frank get one and Lt Lenihan get another. I singled one out and fired a couple of bursts at him before he caught fire, but when

Ready for a pre-dawn takeoff from Cercola, Capt Louis Frank climbs aboard his P-47D 42-75962 in the spring of 1944 (*Author's collection*)

it did start to burn, there was nothing that would have put it out. It hit the ground a mass of flames. I did see one man jump and his parachute open before it started its last spin. I only had the opportunity to fire at one other bomber, and there were plenty of hits on it as many pieces flew off, but it wouldn't burn and I lost it before the job could be finished.'

Lt John Lenihan, who was flying on Maj Chamberlain's wing, had gone after the section of five aeroplanes. He ultimately enjoyed the best luck of all the pilots in the flight, downing three BR.20Ms;

'I followed my leader down and then got in on the fun. One of the bombers was right in front of me so I pulled the trigger and the aeroplane was soon in flames, spinning into the ground. I then banked to the left and another one was in my sights, and with a short burst he too was set on fire and sent crashing to the ground in a mass of flames. I had to look around a bit for the third one, but after locating him, it didn't take long to finish him off. He caught fire like the first one and spun in. I've never seen anything like it. By that time there were no more to be found, so the only thing left to do was to get back into formation and come home.'

Weather limited operations for the remainder of the week, which allowed the 66th time to move from Cercola and rejoin the group. All three squadrons began flying missions from Alto on 10 April, and the day's work accounted for six locomotives of mixed types destroyed, 40 wagons either damaged or destroyed, 27 motor transports of mixed types (the majority camouflaged in light green paint) destroyed, one armoured vehicle destroyed and nine major rail cuts. Capt Marvin Parkhurst, who was the 65th's historical officer, commented that 'if this keeps up, every pilot will have 100 missions or more and be on their way home. These kinds of operations sure keep the crews going, and they sure are doing a good job of it with plenty of spirit'.

The pace only quickened from there. 12 April saw the 57th FG fly eight missions, totalling 116 sorties (including the group's first mission over southern France). The day's most successful mission, flown by the 66th FS, accounted for the destruction of a series of ammunition and fuel dumps. Seven huge explosions were caused, the largest of which sent flames shooting more than 500 ft up into the air and was heard by other group pilots over two miles away at 4000 ft. One of these dumps had a series of five camouflaged 10,000-gallon steel storage tanks that were at least partially destroyed.

The mission's highlight, however, was squadron commander William Benedict's skillful bomb aiming, skip-bombing a 1000-lb bomb into a railway tunnel. The resulting explosion completely destroyed the tunnel, causing flames to shoot out both sides and out of the collapsing top of the tunnel.

There was a similar display two days later when 57th aeroplanes bombed their assigned targets and then shot up every moving train or motor transport they encountered. 64th pilots had another opportunity to engage the Luftwaffe, and they acquitted themselves well despite facing odds of two-to-one. Three Bf 109s were destroyed, with Capt Carll getting two and Lt McCarthy one, with a probable for Lt G P Neese, for the loss of Carll's wingman, Lt Neal Gunderson, who became a PoW.

The remainder of April continued at a rapid pace for the 57th's squadrons. Several leadership changes occurred in the last two weeks of

64th FS CO Maj Art Exon flew his last combat mission in the P-47 on 20 April 1944 when the secondary explosion from the ammunition depot he had just bombed severely damaged his aeroplane. Exon bailed out and was captured, and he spent the remainder of the war at *Stalag Luft* III (*Author's collection*)

As *Strangle* began in earnest, nothing that moved on the roads was safe. Here, a Wehrmacht fuel truck has been caught in the open at Arezzo and strafed by Thunderbolts (*USAF World War 2 Collection*)

the month, beginning with the loss of Maj Art Exon, the 64th's CO, on the 18th. Exon flew through the secondary explosion on a bomb run, which set his aeroplane on fire. He successfully bailed out and was taken prisoner.

Maj William J 'Jeeter' Yates returned to the 57th as its deputy CO on the 22nd. Yates had been one of the initial group of 57th pilots that landed in North Africa in mid-1942, and he had returned to the group to fly a second combat tour.

As April came to a close, the 57th received word that the unit had been rewarded its third Presidential Unit Citation for 'pioneering in the adaptation of the high-altitude P-47 as a low-level strafing and dive-bombing aircraft.' In April alone, its pilots had expended 1,346,500 lbs of bombs and 583,899 rounds of 0.50-cal ammunition in 1702 sorties. The unit's performance throughout the month far exceeded all expectations, averaging twice the required number of ordered sorties nearly every day as an indispensible component of *Strangle*.

While the objective of *Strangle* was to choke off the German means of supply, the secondary effects of the operation became its greatest success. German frontline units continued to get essential supplies both by train and motor transport, although critical items like gasoline were strictly rationed. Allied planners saw motor transport, supply depots and trains as secondary in importance to the destruction of railway infrastructure. However, P-47s made moving supplies during the day a very hazardous venture, and the hundreds of destroyed trains and motor vehicles that littered the Italian countryside stood as a mute testament to the campaign's effectiveness. MAAF's official history records;

'By 11 May, they had destroyed an estimated 800 vehicles and damaged close to 1000. Although the Germans supplanted their own motor transport with several thousand requisitioned Italian vehicles, by the end of *Strangle*, the destruction wrought by MAAF's aeroplanes, together with overuse and inadequate repairs, had taken such a heavy toll that the enemy's road transport was incapable of handling the demands of both the forward and rear zones of communication.'

In addition to restricting German logistical movement, one of the unintended results of the campaign was a significant drain in manpower for the repair effort. German forces rapidly repaired many bridges and

tunnels, but were forced to work at night under extremely stressful conditions, often to see their repairs destroyed by more 500-lb bombs the following morning. By tying up significant manpower reserves in the repair process, many units tasked with repair work were often exhausted by the time they rotated back into the frontline. There is no clear date when *Strangle* officially ended, but working in conjunction with ground forces, Operation *Diadem* began where it left off on 11 May.

DIADEM, ROME AND THE ARNO

May brought changes in both locale and command to the 79th FG. With its move from Capodichino to Pomigliano, the group now had a much longer concrete runway equipped with concrete taxiways that made it easier for the Thunderbolts to taxi with a 2500-lb bomb load. Col Earl Bates relinquished command of the 79th in order to head up the 86th FG and bring it into the P-47 era. His replacement, Col Charles W Stark, a 1937 graduate of West Point, had a strong background with the P-47, having served as the Officer in Charge for Fighter Development at Orlando Field. He had also spent time at the Republic plant in Farmingdale, New York, on the P-47 project. Unfortunately, Stark's command of the 79th lasted just a week.

On 7 May Col Stark took off leading 'Red' section in an 86th FS train-busting mission near Civitavecchia. The flight located two trains of 15 and ten wagons each and dropped 28 500-lb bombs, destroying more than a dozen wagons and cutting the rail line in four separate places. However, flak in the area was both intense and accurate, and Col Stark, flying brand new P-47D 42-25660, coded 'X01', took a hit to his engine on pulling out from his bomb run. Calling the local ground controller 'Grubstake', he advised that he had a dead engine and planned to ditch his aeroplane at the mouth of the Tiber River. He then ordered that no one in the flight was to follow him down or to stay in the area.

Immediately after the remainder of the flight returned to base, a search flight was launched to locate Col Stark and Lt Stafford, who had also fallen to flak. The former's aeroplane was positively identified by its side number five miles north of the mouth of the Tiber in shallow water. It was evident that he had made a normal water landing and that the aeroplane's canopy was open, indicating he had gotten out alive. Col Stark managed to evade capture for three days before being picked up by an enemy patrol. With Stark listed as missing in action, Maj Melvin Nielsen, who had led the 86th FS for the preceding six months, assumed command of the group for the coming offensive.

Operation *Diadem* was a new combined air/ground campaign launched in an effort to join II Corps, held up at the 'Gustav line', with VI Corps, which faced a stalemate on the Anzio beachhead. The air component for the most part continued the destruction of Italian railway infrastructure and any means of transportation available to the German 10th and 14th Armies. However, air units, would now be more closely tied in to advancing ground units providing better air support as the US Fifth and British Eighth Armies pushed the advance.

Six weeks of the constant destruction of Axis trains, motor transport and nearly anything that moved had taken its toll. While German

Col Earl Bates commanded both the 79th and 86th FGs during his time in the MTO. Bates flew more than 200 missions between 1942 and 1945 with both groups in the Warhawk and Thunderbolt (*USAF World War 2 Collection*)

Direct hits with 500-lb GP bombs are evident in this photograph of a destroyed train in northern Italy. At least one direct hit on the tracks cut the railway line, while two near misses inflicted further damage to the train (*USAF World War 2 Collection*)

units still had ammunition and provisions in most cases, gasoline was strictly rationed, paralysing two field armies that relied on mobility in both attack and defence. As the Allied armies jumped off on *Diadem's* initial push northward on 12 May, they ran into resistance that was much stronger than anticipated. After three days of intense fighting with minimal Allied gains, German resistance collapsed and the retreat began.

As a result the 79th FG partially shifted its focus away from just railway infrastructure and began hitting road bridges and any motor transport fleeing northwards. Operating northeast of Rome, 15 P-47s of the 85th FS were wheels-up at 0515 hrs on 15 May looking for bridges and vehicles on the 10th Army main avenue of retreat. Arriving over Foligno at 0615 hrs and moving southeast into the 14th Army sector, the unit was on the hunt. They carried no bombs, relying solely on the firepower of the eight 0.50-cals in their wings to get the job done.

Instead of the standard 'box-four' formation, the 85th spread out into four flights of four aeroplanes line-abreast just 100 ft above the ground for better coverage. The first group of vehicles did not stand a chance, and 17 various types were quickly left in flames, while another 12 were severely damaged. Flak over the vehicle formations was intense, and two of the aeroplanes took hits but kept flying.

The 85th returned to Pomigliano at 0745 hrs, minus one P-47 which landed at Nettuno due to damage received in the attack. The entire 16-ship squadron was outbound for their next target by 1000 hrs, however. Its objective was to choke off road traffic heading north on the eastern side of Lake Bolsano by bombing a road bridge outside of Acquapedente. Weather prevented the flight from reaching its primary target, so a similar road bridge further south was bombed instead, with three direct hits on the southern approach and the remainder well within the target area.

The 86th took off after its sister squadron and was able to get through to the Acquapedente bridge, where pilots dropped 30 1000-lb bombs, putting a 20-ft hole in the span and cratering both the northern and southern approaches. That afternoon, the 87th FS took off with 32 1000-lb bombs underwing to add to the destruction in Acquapedente, but it encountered a flight of 15 Bf 109s and five Fw 190s en route, forcing half of the formation to jettison their bombs and tangle with the enemy;

'As our formation went into its bomb run, 20-30 Me 109s engaged', noted the squadron's operations report. 'One section kept the enemy fighters occupied while the remainder of the formation attacked the bridges – a good bombing pattern was secured and both bridges are believed unserviceable. Three enemy fighters were destroyed and one probably destroyed. One of our aircraft sustained hits and the pilot was forced to land at Anzio with slight injuries. A gratifying result of this engagement was the discovery that a P-47, not considered a low altitude aircraft, can manoeuvre advantageously with Me 109s almost on the deck, even though under the handicap of being on a bomb run.'

Lts Damon Adkins and Walter Petermann both downed Bf 109s. All 12 1000-lb bombs dropped were well within the target area, including three direct hits on the bridge, despite the presence of enemy fighters.

The 79th's operational pace continued to accelerate over the next week-and-a-half. As the 10th and 14th Armies retreated northwards, XII TAC missions moved farther south to support the advancing Allied armies and to catch as many retreating vehicles, horse carts, bicycles and other methods of transportation in the open as possible.

As the US II and VI Corps drew together on 24 May, the 86th FS set several new records for a fighter-bomber unit. The day's first mission left at 0540 hrs as the 86th headed out to strafe a target of opportunity. En route, it linked up with a tactical reconnaissance F-6 Mustang from the 111th TRS that guided the unit onto a train of 30 wagons near Riano, north of Rome. The P-47 pilots roared in from 1000 ft and dropped 20 1000-lb bombs onto the target, demolishing it and the rails beneath it.

Once the flight was no longer encumbered by bombs, it was free to hunt for targets of opportunity en route back to Pomigliano. Due to the enemy's retreat in complete disarray, it was not long before the 86th found 20 vehicles that tried to disperse once they were sighted. The 0.50-cal machine guns made quick work of the soft-skinned vehicles, leaving 17 of them in flames as they headed home.

The 86th's third mission of the day unfolded similarly to the first, the squadron's 12 aeroplanes rendezvousing with an RAF Spitfire that guided them to an enemy tank concentration near Arce, northwest of Cassino. Some 22 1000-lb bombs were dropped on the tanks, with ten direct hits and 12 near misses. Explosions from the five tanks that were confirmed destroyed reached more than 1000 ft in the air. With no bombs left, the unit again strafed targets of opportunity en route back to refuel and rearm, this time catching a six-gun 40 mm flak battery unaware, silencing all six weapons and leaving its ammunition truck a burning hulk.

In 14 hours of continuous operation, the 79th flew 12 complete missions, totalling 156 sorties, with an average mission length of one hour and 45 minutes. The missions flown ran the gamut from armed reconnaissance, strafing, CAS and railway busting to aerial combat (although no claims were credited and the German fighters only made a single pass). Some 306 1000-lb bombs were dropped on targets during that time (ten were jettisoned on various missions due to flak damage) – a greater tonnage than most heavy bomb groups would drop in one day.

Meanwhile, the 27th FG's 524th FS flew its first combat mission in the P-47 over the Anzio beachhead as the crescendo built to a roar on the Italian peninsula. Switching from the P-40 to the P-47 had been an extended process, since the group continued to fly combat missions in the Warhawk while transitioning to the Thunderbolt. The 524th's maintainers performed no shortage of miracles keeping two complete sets of aircraft flight-ready during the transition period.

On 19 May the 524th encountered heavy flak at 8500 ft over Fondi while inbound to its target. Flight leader Capt Arthur 'Red' Sortore was on his 115th combat mission when his P-47 was badly hit, forcing him to bail out five miles north of Fondi – then almost 15 miles behind enemy lines. He landed safely, and although a few Germans shot at him as he neared the ground, he was able to find cover and hide out until nightfall. Evading enemy patrols for almost two days, Sortore headed south until he made contact with advancing US forces north of Itri.

Prior to this point, P-47 integration with advancing ground units had been limited. CAS was a 'third phase' priority, behind achievement of air superiority and interdiction of enemy supply routes. Now as the Fifth and Eighth Armies assaulted northward, the Thunderbolt was finally being proven as the USAAF's best CAS aeroplane. The pilots of the 524th, operating over the Anzio beachhead, may have been the first to use the P-47 in the CAS role, and the successes of their first week of operations were tempered by the loss of four pilots and aircraft.

'Flak was not much heavier than usual, but due to the fact that the unit was pressing its attacks very aggressively and also because a large amount of strafing was done, the enemy downed more of our aeroplanes during this period than at any time in the past ten months', noted the 524th's operations report. 'Seventeen P-47s were damaged by flak and four lost. Three of the pilots of the lost fighters bailed out and returned to base. Two of these, Capt Arthur Sortore and Lt James Pribil, came through enemy lines safely. The fourth, Capt Benjamin L Rorie, our CO, was killed by a direct flak hit while strafing tanks and trucks.'

The 27th FG, and specifically the 524th FS, contributed significantly to the destruction of the fleeing elements of the 14th Army. In ten days of operations, the 524th claimed 132 trucks, 15 tanks, two armoured cars, seven guns of various calibre, three motorcycles and more than 100 wagons destroyed or damaged. The First Special Service Force (the famed US/Canadian commando outfit) witnessed the 27th in action firsthand and corroborated many of these claims. According to its unit history, on 25 May 'the air was thick with allied bombers and fighters attacking the heavily travelled German escape route up and down the North-South road through the Velletri Gap. In a heavy two-day schedule of air attacks on the retiring 14th Army, the USAAF claimed 1050 enemy cars, trucks and tanks destroyed – a bag that was confirmed by ground count'.

The 524th had its first tangle with enemy fighters on the afternoon of 26 May when eight P-47s attacked retreating German tanks and motor transport southeast of Lake Bracciano. Twenty enemy fighters attacked from 15,000 ft, damaging two Thunderbolts in their first pass. Lt Elmer Carroll was able to score good hits on a Bf 109 before having his rudder cables shot out, forcing him to leave the fight, while Lt Harold Hamner's P-47D 42-74999 got so badly shot up that he was forced to bail out. However, the tables quickly turned and the enemy formation broke contact, but not before Lt Robert LaFollette damaged another Bf 109 and Lt Clyde Brown destroyed an Fw 190. As the P-47s disengaged, two Spitfires dove on the fleeing Germans and the 524th pilots were able to confirm the destruction of two additional Fw 190s.

While the 79th and the 524th were flying close interdiction and air support as the Allied offensive pushed northwards, the 57th continued to operate strictly in the interdiction role from Corsica at an operational tempo similar to the other two units. On 25 May – the group's most intense day – the 66th FS increased its air-to-air and air-to-ground scores significantly. Upon crossing the shoreline south of Tarquinia at 7000 ft, the flight located and bombed a three-span railway bridge, holing it with several direct hits, but failing to drop the bridge entirely.

Heading north at 500 ft, the flight split into two elements of six P-47s apiece. Squadron CO Maj Benedict took one, and the second was led by 1Lt George Kriss. As they looked for targets of opportunity, the flight was jumped by eight Fw 190s of I./SG 4 that had taken off from Canino airfield to intercept them. The fighters came in from the 'seven o'clock' position, and Lt Kriss dove his formation under the Fw 190s to gain some airspeed for the fight. He then turned through 180 degrees and immediately had two Focke-Wulfs in his sights. Opening fire, Kriss followed both aircraft down until they hit the ground. Lt Edwin Flood then fired a 30-degree deflection shot at another Fw 190, seeing pieces fly off the aeroplane around the canopy area before it too crashed.

Lt William Ehney manoeuvred quickly, seeing another Focke-Wulf making a 180-degree turn that would bring it right onto his tail. Ehney pulled through the turn faster and fired at the Fw 190, scoring multiple hits. At 500 ft and nearly 400 mph, the stricken Focke-Wulf hit the ground almost immediately. Lt Robert Kaiser was the last of the flight to score, shooting up an Fw 190 and leaving it smoking badly.

While the 66th FS gave better than it got, two P-47s failed to return home. After the flight had separated into two elements, Maj Benedict's element took intense antiaircraft fire and Lt Mervin Hitchcock's aeroplane (P-47D 42-75659) suffered catastrophic flak damage as he flew on his CO's wing looking for targets. Hitchcock bailed out and was taken prisoner. Meanwhile, Lt William Dickinson, in Lt Kriss' element, was hit in the initial bounce by the Fw 190s. Mortally wounded, he bailed out of his stricken P-47D but succumbed to his injuries shortly thereafter.

Mission tempo subsided after 26 May, and most P-47 units in XII TAC dropped to three or even two daily missions over the next few days. On Corsica, the 57th received two new fighters on the 27th – 'they are both "silver", or unpainted, and one is the latest model P-47. This ship has a "bubble" canopy and this and other changes in the fuselage give it a different appearance than that of the older models. The aircraft was purchased by employees of Republic, and it bears an inscription on the side and the number "45"', noted the group's operations report.

ROME

With Fifth Army's two corps now operating together as a whole army again, the drive to Rome became a sprint. However, instead of pursuing the retreating enemy, Fifth Army commander Gen Mark Clark shifted his axis of attack in order to capture Rome, and thus claim the first Axis capital city to be liberated. Reconnaissance elements of the 1st Armored Division were the first US units within the city limits in the early hours of 4 June, and shortly thereafter, the First Special Service Force became the first Allied unit into the heart of the city.

The first 'bubbletop' Thunderbolt delivered to the 57th FG was P-47D 42-26421, which was also the 45th war-bond Thunderbolt purchased by the workers at the Republic Farmingdale plant. Unfortunately it only saw brief service with the 66th FS before 2Lt Thomas Davis failed to return from a dive-bombing mission in it on 2 September 1944 (*Author's Collection*)

DIADEM, ROME AND THE ARNO

35

During the rapid advance on Rome, air-to-ground and ground-to-air communication was found to be sorely lacking. Requests for CAS had to go up to corps level and then be sent through channels to supporting aviation elements, wasting precious time and potentially costing friendly lives. The speed of the advance in the last week of May also caught supporting aviation units off guard, and with friendly ground units not where they were expected to be, friendly fire incidents resulted.

In order to reduce the potential for the latter, and quicken the reaction time for XII TAC fighter-bombers, two systems arose to better direct inbound aircraft. 'Rover Joe' teams had been operating since the Sicilian campaign, but with the massive increase in fighter-bomber operations during the push to Rome, additional teams were created to better direct XII TAC's fighters. A 'Rover Joe' team normally consisted of a fighter pilot, a ground officer and an enlisted radio operator/driver. Once fighters hit their primary targets, they would check in with 'Grubstake', 'Acorn' or one of the other sector controllers, who then handed them over to a 'Rover Joe' team for direction to targets of opportunity. The latter, in a Jeep (fitted with an SCR-522 radio to talk to the fighters and an SCR-191 long range radio for communication with higher HQ) near the battlefield, would talk the aircraft in on a target. By utilising fighter pilots in the 'Rover Joe' role, common language and understanding of the aircraft's capabilities greatly eased air/ground cooperation, and made for a more efficient engagement of time-essential targets.

The other method began as something specific only to the 1st Armored Division, where the latter's three L-5 spotter aircraft, nicknamed 'Horseflies', were outfitted with USAAF High Frequency (HF) radios that enabled them to talk directly to P-40s or P-47s operating in their sector. If no fighter-bombers were in the air, the L-5 pilot would report back to the division artillery fire direction centre, which would then pass on the mission request through channels. Once the mission was accepted, inbound P-47 pilots would call in on the L-5's frequency and get talked onto the target by the airborne 'Horsefly' controller. The system worked effectively until the division reached the Arno in late July, at which point the USAAF reclaimed the loaned HF radios in order to adopt a similar system using its own liaison squadrons.

The system was used to great effect on the morning of 5 June when the 524th was sent to cut the railway line between Orte and Capranica. Once the flight had dropped its bombs the pilots contacted 'Grubstake' for targets of opportunity and were vectored south of Monteresi and east of Lake Bracciano. At 0845 hrs they linked up with a 'Horsefly' controller who led them to a good release point to initiate their strafing attacks on a vehicle concentration. Apparently, the enemy unit had been travelling by night and had just pulled off the road as the sun was coming up.

65th FS P-47 pilot Lt Martin McGilvary was photographed during his rotation to the frontlines as a 'Rover Joe'. By the early autumn of 1944, Thunderbolt units were rotating experienced pilots up to the frontlines to facilitate CAS missions (*USAF World War 2 Collection*)

First conducted with 324th FG P-40s, an L-5 'Horsefly' airborne controller forms up with a flight of 314th FS Warhawks. The 'Horsefly' was routinely flown by a P-40 or P-47 pilot over the frontlines to direct fighter-bombers onto targets of opportunity in their Area of Operations (*USAF World War 2 Collection*)

The 524th pilots sighted approximately 50 trucks parked under the trees along the side of the road. All had been travelling northbound when they pulled off. Antiaircraft fire consisted mostly of small arms and light machine guns, but it was fairly intense and accurate. Lt Robert LaFollette's aeroplane took some hits while strafing, eventually causing him and his wingman, Lt Shank, to divert to Nettuno. The squadron claimed seven 'flamers', one destroyed and 16 damaged. Once LaFollette and Shank returned to the unit later in the day, an additional four trucks destroyed and two damaged were added to the day's tally.

The 522nd FS completed its transition period and flew its first combat mission (a nine-ship armed reconnaissance mission from Civita Castellana to Orte, Orvieto, Todi and Rieti) that same day. Hunting was good on its first mission, the flight strafing a number of vehicles, destroying a tank and eight trucks and leaving another six damaged. More than 50 horse-drawn artillery pieces were also spotted but they were not attacked as they appeared to be within the bomb safe line.

The 27th remained at Santa Maria airfield, on the mainland, through to mid July. The 523rd did not fly its first combat mission until 23 June, and the weather refused to cooperate, thus making it a day of frustration. After two failed attempts to reach a specific railway junction, the eight-P-47 formation diverted to a secondary target farther down the line, where six of 16 500-lb bombs found their marks, cutting the rails in several places. After dropping its bombs, the flight reconnoitred the line, locating and strafing a string of wagons, damaging ten.

SHIFTING FOCUS

Developments in France two days after the liberation of Rome caused a major shift in XII TAC planning that had a twofold effect. Firstly, it accelerated the remaining XII TAC fighter groups' transition to the P-47, and secondly, it shifted fighter-bomber basing for the coming operations. Airfields like Pomigliano and Ciampino were well within range of targets around Rome, but as the Fifth and Eighth Armies drove towards the Arno River, they risked moving out of the P-47's operational range.

Corsica, however, was vital for future operations. The 57th FG had already proven that interdiction of vital targets on both the Italian and French mainland was feasible from Corsican airfields, and the upcoming invasion of Southern France would require significant air power to support VI Corps' assault. As has been recorded in numerous volumes prior to this, after the fall of Rome and the Allied invasion of Normandy, Italy became of secondary importance to the Allied war effort. By expanding the targeting focus of *Strangle/Diadem*, XII TAC would be able, in theory, to interdict German supply lines and infrastructure in southern France and also hit the shortened enemy logistics train in Italy.

Fighters flying from Corsican bases had roughly 100 miles of the Tyrrhenian Sea to cross before reaching mainland Italy. Well within the P-47's effective combat radius, southern France was nearly twice that distance from Alto, Serragia, and Ghisonaccia. Poretta, on the west coast, was only slightly closer. However, the 79th, still flying from Pomigliano, near Naples, became increasingly distant from the frontlines, and in the second week of June the group moved to Serragia. The air echelon arrived on 11 June and began combat operations the following morning.

79th pilots, used to plush quarters at Pomigliano, found themselves living in a crowded tent village a mile from the airfield. With a skeleton crew manning the group's non-flying sections, many complained about the food and the speed at which the 'literally mile-long chow line' moved.

The first missions from Serragia shifted focus back to destroying any infrastructure that the German armies in Italy could benefit from using. Bridge- and train-busting was the name of the game, and the standard two 12-ship missions per day became the norm once again. While personnel of the 79th were getting used to their new surroundings, and waiting anxiously for the remainder of the group to arrive, the 57th continued to fly interdiction missions in the region south and east of Pisa.

Both groups, however, were called to action over the island of Elba on 16-17 June as Free French forces met stiff resistance in the fight to take the island of Napoleon's exile. Primarily serving as on-call CAS for French troops, both units strafed and bombed gun positions, blockhouses, ammunition dumps and several flak ships and S-100 class E-boats as they covered both the invading Frenchmen and the flotilla supporting the invasion. By the 18th, the island was in French hands.

Two days later, as 12 P-47s of the 87th FS were taxiing out on another bridge-busting mission, a flash target cancelled the operation. Reconnaissance flights over Genoa had identified the Italian aircraft carrier *Aquila* moored in the harbour under camouflage nets, flying the German ensign. The P-47s were hastily reloaded with 500-lb bombs, which would be plenty for the job at hand. One pilot aborted just after takeoff when his gear would not retract, but the remaining 11 continued on the 45-minute inbound leg, arriving over Genoa at 1515 hrs.

Spread out line-abreast and roaring in at no greater than 1000 ft, the three waves of 'Thunderbombers', led by Lt Gordon MacMoody, placed their bombs with deadly accuracy. The first two penetrated the starboard bow just above the waterline and exploded, while two more direct hits amidships followed by four bombs on or adjacent to the stern started a blaze within the carrier. More direct hits on the pier to which the vessel was moored resulted in additional fires and a massive explosion. The flak was the most intense seen in months, and Lt Tom Hawk and his P-47 both took hits, forcing him to head home wounded in a barely flyable Thunderbolt. Four P-47s also strafed the flightdeck from bow to stern, but were moving too fast to observe any significant results.

As the flight re-formed and headed back to Corsica, columns of white and black smoke rose from the *Aquila* to an altitude above 1000 ft. Eighteen hours later, a 3rd Photo Group F-5 Lightning made several high altitude passes over Genoa harbour and found the carrier still burning.

While the 57th and 79th FGs were adding to their total tonnage sunk, the 27th continued to support Fifth Army from Ciampino airfield near Rome, although the group's increasing distance from the bomb line was decreasing its effectiveness. The Thunderbolt's combat radius was put to the test on the 29th when a photo-reconnaissance flight located a concentration of nearly 500 wagons loaded with armoured vehicles and gasoline in the Rimini-Forli

Still tied to the pier in Genoa harbour, the Italian aircraft carrier *Aquila* was actually sunk in her berth by the 86th FS's devastatingly accurate dive- and skip-bombing. Although the vessel was raised and repairs were attempted, *Aquila* was effectively out of the war after the squadron's devastating attack (*US Navy*)

area. All three of the group's squadrons flew the 300+ mile trip as a round robin so that once the 523rd had expended its ordnance, the 524th would be overhead, followed by the 522nd shortly thereafter.

According to the 523rd's monthly report, 'the cars were located and very accurately bombed, direct hits being obtained on the train at four separate places. Many cars were left burning and many others damaged as a result of the bombing and fire from the guns of the aircraft. Other bombs were dropped on the rail yards at Forli, two of them direct hits on the tracks and four others landing on a large building believed to be a power station. The building was set on fire and numerous blue explosions were observed, each one creating additional damage. The formation then turned on 30 box cars and a locomotive and damaged every single unit.

'Leaving Forli and continuing along the tracks, an additional 25 box cars were attacked and all of them damaged by strafing, with some of them left burning. Rendering this railroad unusable was a severe loss to the enemy, and certainly interfered with his plans to evacuate personnel and valuable equipment from the battle area.'

Noting the numerous fires already burning, the 524th took over from the 523rd and claimed another 100 wagons damaged or destroyed.

May and June had been a period of transitions. After months of stalemate, the collapse and pursuit of the German Tenth and Fourteenth Armies fleeing northwards after the Anzio breakout (and the subsequent liberation of Rome) had significantly changed the tactical air power situation in the Mediterranean. The P-47 had proven itself to be a dominant force in supporting that advance, both in the air-to-air and air-to-ground roles, and new methods of ground and air control allowed squadrons to more efficiently engage targets of opportunity or necessity.

Yet with the strategic situation in the ETO shifting in favour of the invasion of Normandy on 6 June, the three XII TAC fighter groups flying the P-47 felt the pull of tactical necessity towards southern France.

In order to supply the increasing number of Allied units coming over the beaches at Normandy, more ports would be needed to handle the massive amounts of shipping required to sustain the advance. The port facilities in southern France made more logistical sense than those in Italy, and the threat of landing another Allied Army Group to threaten the left flank of Rommel's Army Group G was sure to pull divisions away from the Normandy beachhead. Yet US and British leaders at the highest levels went back and forth over the necessity of the southern France operation (codenamed *Anvil*) throughout most of June and July.

In the meantime, the 27th FG prepared to move yet again, the first of its P-47s touching down on Corsican soil on 8 July.

In anticipation of this new operation, Corsica had become an American 'aircraft carrier' in the Mediterranean. By the end of July, no fewer than five full Thunderbolt groups would be flying from Corsican airfields.

Unlike many of the Twelfth Air Force's campaigns, Operation *Strangle* did not have an end date or short term victory criteria. The operation would only be deemed completed once every railway line and every highway in Italy had been paralysed by roving P-47s (*USAF World War 2 Collection*)

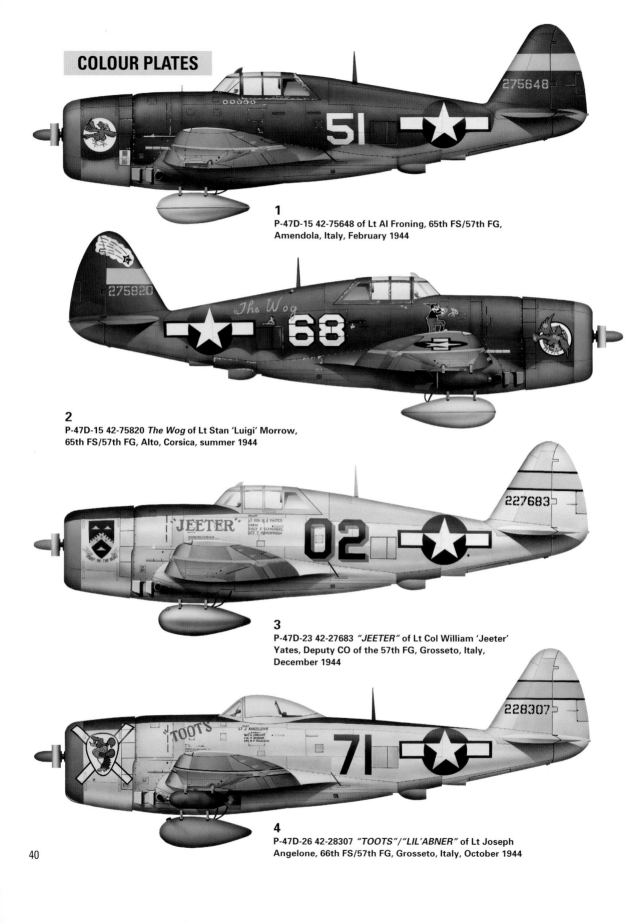

1
P-47D-15 42-75648 of Lt Al Froning, 65th FS/57th FG,
Amendola, Italy, February 1944

2
P-47D-15 42-75820 *The Wog* of Lt Stan 'Luigi' Morrow,
65th FS/57th FG, Alto, Corsica, summer 1944

3
P-47D-23 42-27683 *"JEETER"* of Lt Col William 'Jeeter'
Yates, Deputy CO of the 57th FG, Grosseto, Italy,
December 1944

4
P-47D-26 42-28307 *"TOOTS"/"LIL'ABNER"* of Lt Joseph
Angelone, 66th FS/57th FG, Grosseto, Italy, October 1944

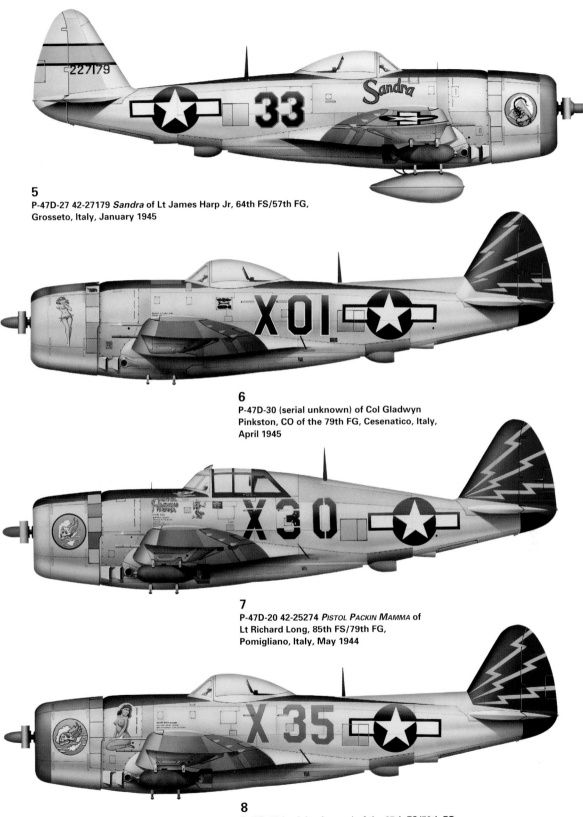

5
P-47D-27 42-27179 *Sandra* of Lt James Harp Jr, 64th FS/57th FG,
Grosseto, Italy, January 1945

6
P-47D-30 (serial unknown) of Col Gladwyn
Pinkston, CO of the 79th FG, Cesenatico, Italy,
April 1945

7
P-47D-20 42-25274 *Pistol Packin Mamma* of
Lt Richard Long, 85th FS/79th FG,
Pomigliano, Italy, May 1944

8
P-47D-40 (serial unknown) of the 85th FS/79th FG,
Cesenatico, Italy, April 1945

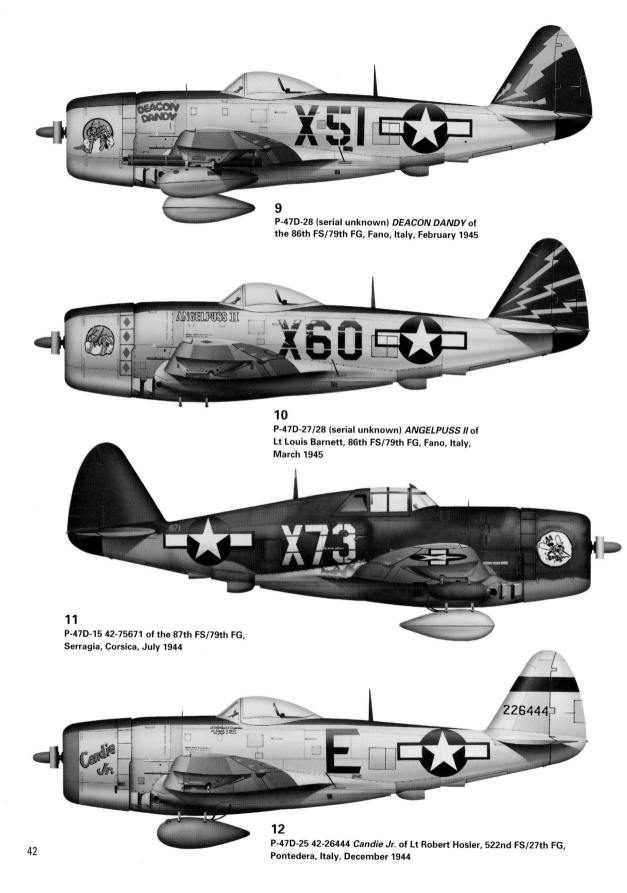

9
P-47D-28 (serial unknown) *DEACON DANDY* of
the 86th FS/79th FG, Fano, Italy, February 1945

10
P-47D-27/28 (serial unknown) *ANGELPUSS II* of
Lt Louis Barnett, 86th FS/79th FG, Fano, Italy,
March 1945

11
P-47D-15 42-75671 of the 87th FS/79th FG,
Serragia, Corsica, July 1944

12
P-47D-25 42-26444 *Candie Jr.* of Lt Robert Hosler, 522nd FS/27th FG,
Pontedera, Italy, December 1944

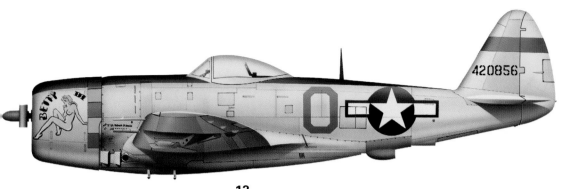

13
P-47D-30 44-20856 *BETTY III* of 1Lt Robert Jones,
522nd FS/27th FG, Heilbronn, Germany, 2 April 1945

14
P-47D-27/28 (serial unknown) of Lt Irwin Lebow,
524th FS/27th FG, Pontedera, Italy, 8 February 1945

15
P-47D-28 42-28604 *DORA PAT III* of Lt Col George Lee,
deputy CO of the 86th FG, Pisa, Italy, October 1944

16
P-47D-30 44-20863 *Lois* of Lt John Brink, 525th FS/86th FG,
Grosseto, Italy, 25 December 1944

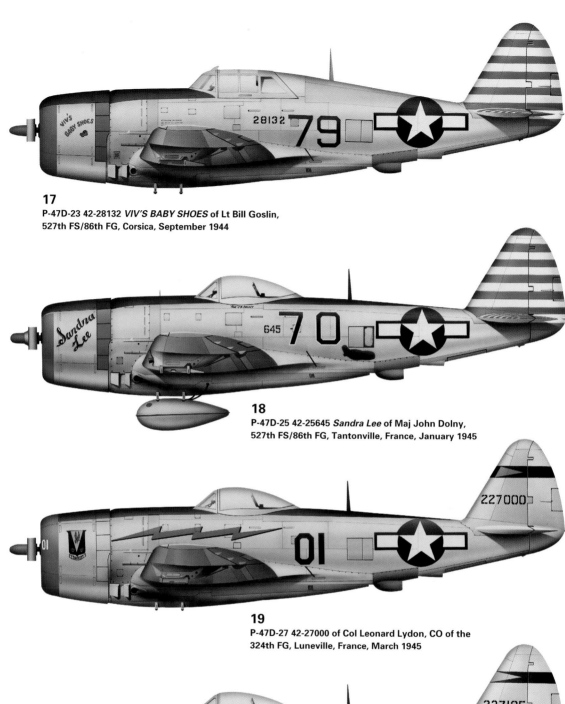

17
P-47D-23 42-28132 *VIV'S BABY SHOES* of Lt Bill Goslin,
527th FS/86th FG, Corsica, September 1944

18
P-47D-25 42-25645 *Sandra Lee* of Maj John Dolny,
527th FS/86th FG, Tantonville, France, January 1945

19
P-47D-27 42-27000 of Col Leonard Lydon, CO of the
324th FG, Luneville, France, March 1945

20
P-47D-27 42-27105 of Lt Stan Hart, 314th FS/324th FG, Ghisonaccia,
Corsica, August 1944

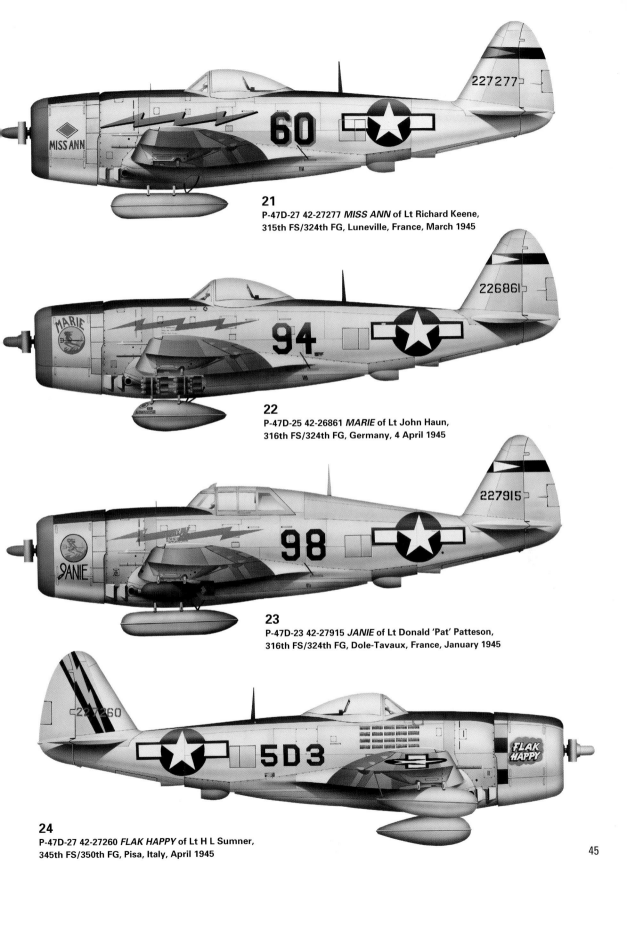

21
P-47D-27 42-27277 *MISS ANN* of Lt Richard Keene,
315th FS/324th FG, Luneville, France, March 1945

22
P-47D-25 42-26861 *MARIE* of Lt John Haun,
316th FS/324th FG, Germany, 4 April 1945

23
P-47D-23 42-27915 *JANIE* of Lt Donald 'Pat' Patteson,
316th FS/324th FG, Dole-Tavaux, France, January 1945

24
P-47D-27 42-27260 *FLAK HAPPY* of Lt H L Sumner,
345th FS/350th FG, Pisa, Italy, April 1945

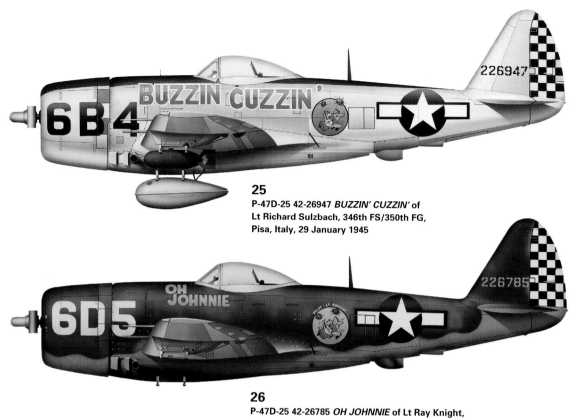

25
P-47D-25 42-26947 *BUZZIN' CUZZIN'* of
Lt Richard Sulzbach, 346th FS/350th FG,
Pisa, Italy, 29 January 1945

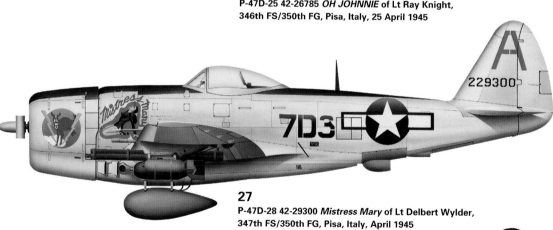

26
P-47D-25 42-26785 *OH JOHNNIE* of Lt Ray Knight,
346th FS/350th FG, Pisa, Italy, 25 April 1945

27
P-47D-28 42-29300 *Mistress Mary* of Lt Delbert Wylder,
347th FS/350th FG, Pisa, Italy, April 1945

28
P-47D-25 42-26756 of Tenente Alberto Martins Torres,
1st BFS/350th FG, Pisa, Italy, spring 1945

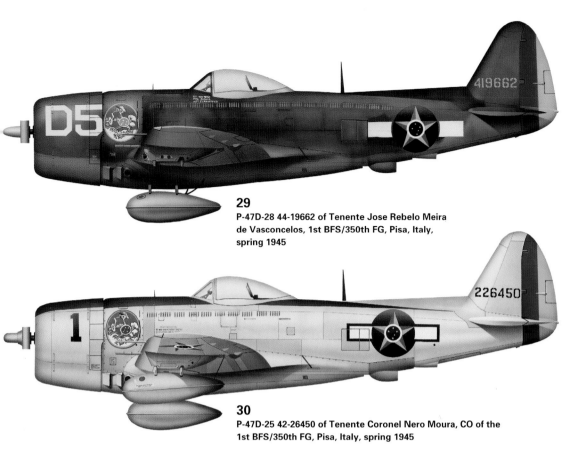

29
P-47D-28 44-19662 of Tenente Jose Rebelo Meira
de Vasconcelos, 1st BFS/350th FG, Pisa, Italy,
spring 1945

30
P-47D-25 42-26450 of Tenente Coronel Nero Moura, CO of the
1st BFS/350th FG, Pisa, Italy, spring 1945

When Lt Col George Lee took command of the 86th FG in February 1945, the group universally adopted
a new identity as 'Lee's Lieutenants', taking their name from the popular Civil War history published
two years prior

SOUTHERN FRANCE

The American shift in focus was obvious throughout the MTO, and a source of great controversy between Allied leaders. While British planners wanted to continue the Italian Front as the focus of the southern drive on Nazi Germany, the US plan to invade southern France intended to capture the ports of Toulon, Marseilles and Nice to facilitate the faster delivery of men and materiel to what was seen as the main thrust to liberate Europe.

The US Army's VI Corps (consisting of the 3rd, 36th and 45th Infantry Divisions and the First Special Service Force) had already been withdrawn from the frontlines and was refitting and undergoing an intense refresher on amphibious operations in the Naples area. Similarly, nearly every USAAF tactical air asset in Italy had been moved, or was in the process of moving, to Corsica. Italian civilians talked openly about the upcoming operation in southern France, and even German PoWs knew that the next significant offensive would be on the French Riviera. However, Fifth Army ground operations continued north of Rome, where the US IV Corps moved into positions on Fifth Army's western flank. The sprint to destroy the retreating German 10th and 14th Armies had slowed, and facing new Axis defensive lines, the Fifth's divisions again were forced to fight for every yard gained.

In the air, July added six more Bf 109s to the tally of the 66th FS. The squadron, operating nearly at its maximum combat radius, bombed a railway bridge in the town of Bondeno, close to Italy's eastern coast. While the span remained intact, 25 500-lb bombs cut the tracks on either side of the bridge. The flight turned northbound and strafed 15 wagons in the Bondeno marshalling yard, before turning back westbound and following the canal southeast of the town. Four barges were strafed and left smoking as they left the area. Climbing back to altitude to conserve fuel on the route back, the unit skirted south of the Luftwaffe airfield at Reggio and sighted 14 Bf 109s in two flights at 4000 ft and 6000 ft.

Flying P-47 '91', 2Lt William Hill led the squadron into attack, breaking up both enemy formations. Hill's aeroplane took some damage as he led the way, but the unit gave far worse than it received. Flying in the No 3 position in Hill's section, Lt Claude Rahn was first to score, claiming a single Bf 109 destroyed. The second section, however, tore the Messerschmitts to pieces. Led by Lt Richard Johnson, who claimed one Bf 109 destroyed and two damaged, Lts Thomas Davis (flying Johnson's wing) and Stephen Bettinger each destroyed single Bf 109s. Bringing up the rear of the section, Lt Howard Cleveland destroyed two fighters while protecting the tails of his section mates. All 11 Thunderbolts safely recovered at Alto, with holes in Hill's, Johnson's and Davis' aeroplanes.

Maj Charles Leaf, commander of the 66th FS, poses with his aeroplane, P-47D 42-26843 '75'. Leaf assumed command of the 66th FS on 19 July 1944, and remained CO through to the end of the war. This aircraft was badly damaged during a CAS mission flown in support of the 92nd Infantry Division on 29 December 1944 (*USAF World War 2 Collection*)

Capt Richard Long flew 109 missions in the P-47 between March and October 1944, amassing nearly 250 hours of combat time. He was promoted to captain and became the 85th FS's Assistant Operations officer on 17 September 1944 (*Jackie Kaar*)

Further south, the 85th FS opened the month with two Bf 109s damaged. Capt Eugene Kleiderer and Lts Richard Long and Cecil Bush were on a dive-bombing mission over Italy when they were bounced by enemy fighters. Long and Bush collaborated in damaging one of the Bf 109s and Capt Kleiderer added to his score with one damaged as well. The previous day, unit pilots Benjamin Cassiday (on his first operational mission) and David Shuttleworth each shot a Bf 109 off the other's tail for two confirmed destroyed.

Although XII TAC had moved to Corsica, mission focus continued to be on the Italian mainland. Alto, Poretto and Ghisonaccia, all on the island's east coast, kept even the farthest reaches of Italy well within the Thunderbolt's effective combat radius, and allowed the continuation of *Strangle's* objectives. The effects of this phase of operations were not as spectacular as those obtained during the chaotic withdrawal of the 10th and 14th Armies in May and June, but the continued campaign against German communications and logistical networks kept Kesselring's logistics officers focused on how to avoid roving fighter-bombers, rather than on getting needed supples to their beleaguered troops.

The 57th FG continued to add to the consternation of German logisticians when it attacked fuel dumps north of Parma on 7 July, destroying hundreds of thousands of gallons of fuel vital to 14th Army operations. The group's three squadrons launched at 30-minute intervals, with the 64th taking the lead. The 'Black Scorpions'' target had erroneously been reported as a fuel dump, but it actually appeared to be a supply point. Against scant flak opposition over the target, the P-47s released their bombs from 1500 ft, collapsing two warehouses and demolishing two other buildings. The remainder of the unit's bombs fell among supply crates outside the buildings, but due to their non-explosive nature it was difficult to assess the amount of damage actually caused.

As the 'Scorpions'' were headed home, the 65th arrived on-target and unleashed its destruction on the German fuel supply. Some 24 bombs fell within the target area and started a massive firestorm that created a column of black smoke that reached 6000 ft. The 65th did not encounter any enemy opposition, but several suspect radio calls were made warning of inbound enemy aircraft. None, however, were sighted, and the radio calls were therefore assumed to be hostile attempts to get the formation to jettison its bombs prior to initiating its attacks.

The round robin continued with the 66th bombing on cue from its flight leader. Five large tanks were seen in the target area, and one was set on fire and another blew up. The unit then strafed the area, blowing up a fuel tanker, trailer and seven trucks, before heading home.

The day's successes continued when, on the 65th's afternoon rail cutting mission, Lt James 'Wabbit' Hare sighted a high-wing Italian Ca.133

bomber heading north at about 150 ft over the Ligurian Sea. Rolling in behind it, he squeezed off a burst that destroyed the three-engined aircraft's right motor and started a fire that ignited the bomber's fuel tanks. The Ca.133 exploded and hit the water. Encounters like this were rare, but significant, as they lessened the potential for night harassment raids on Fifth Army units in the frontline.

According to Fifth Army, there were 'an undetermined number of obsolete German and Italian aircraft of various types that were used mainly for night operations against Allied troops and installations. Some of these training units were based in Yugoslavia and had been in action against the Partisans there, but as the lines progressed northward Allied troops in Italy came within their range'.

Lt James 'Wabbit' Hare poses in the cockpit of his P-47D 42-75719 '44' *WICKED WABBIT* at Alto, on Corsica, in the late spring of 1944. Hare flew this particular Thunderbolt until it was replaced with a 'bubble top' that would also be nicknamed *WICKED WABBIT* (*James Hare collection via 57thfighter group.com/Mark O'Boyle*)

OPERATION *MALLORY MAJOR*

With the Germans entrenched between the Arno and Po rivers, Twelfth Air Force planners devised an operation to further constrict supplies to the two armies. Maj William Mallory in Twelfth Air Force HQ realised that all of the essential supplies that those armies needed had to 'funnel through some two-dozen rail and road spans'. By destroying all of the bridges along the Po from the Ligurian to the Adriatic Sea, it would be possible to starve the Tenth and Fourteenth Armies into submission. Fifth Army was not impressed with the plan, hoping to eventually use those bridges on the drive northwards, but since both the US Fifth and British Eighth Armies were pausing at the Arno the operation made sense;

'On 10 July Allied Armies Italy (AAI) ordered the bombing of bridges across the Po River. It had been hoped some of these bridges might be captured intact when Fifth and Eighth Armies entered the Po Valley, but by that date it had become apparent that a rapid breakthrough to such a depth was impossible. Bombers and fighter-bombers, turned loose in the valley, rapidly knocked out many of the bridges, and by the end of July the USAAF reported principal rail routes across northern Italy from the French frontier to the Adriatic Sea had been cut at least temporarily. Bridges, railways and roads closer to the frontlines were also blasted.'

While the operation primarily used the Twelfth's B-25s and B-26s starting on the morning of 12 July, XII TAC's P-47s were given some respite from interdiction missions by escorting the medium bombers to the Po. Meeting up with 36 B-25s of the 310th BG over Bastia, Corsica, the 65th stayed with the bombers for the entire uneventful trip. The target was obscured by a smoke screen, so 65th FS pilots were unable to confirm the bombing results. Flak over the target was minor, but on the return leg the B-25s ran into some expected antiaircraft fire over La Spezia. The 57th flew two more escorts on the 12th without incident, giving pilots a welcome change from ground attack.

Phase 1 of Operation *Mallory Major* destroyed or severely damaged every span across the Po within the first 48 hours, cutting off the two German

Armies between the river and the Allied ground forces. Once the medium bombers had dropped those spans, it was up to the fighter-bombers to make sure the bridges stayed down – a job at which XII TAC had become quite adept. Follow-up missions by all three Thunderbolt units occurred throughout the week in an effort to destroy ongoing repairs and discourage further work on restoring the bridges.

The only challenge by the Luftwaffe came on the morning of 13 July when the 86th FS was on escort duty en route to the Po. Capt George Ewing was leading a flight of 12 Thunderbolts southwest of Ferrara when the lead ('Blue') flight was jumped by several Bf 109s. Capt Ewing downed a Bf 109 during the initial bounce (and he would add another to his score on the 19th), while 'Yellow' flight turned into the attacking fighters, chasing one for several miles before returning to the formation. As 'Yellow' flight pulled back into position, flight leader Lt Alan Austin realised he had an extra fighter in his four-ship section. Lt Robert Ryan's P-47D 42-76015 'X53' had taken a direct hit in the oil reservoir, and his machine was now covered in black fluid. Austin recalled;

'Oil was streaming from his cowl flaps in such a manner as to cover all of the left side of his fuselage and half of the right side. His canopy was completely covered. His transmitter was out, but the receiver was okay, so I instructed him to open his canopy, fly close formation with me and signify yes or no to questions I would ask him by nodding his head.'

Ryan nodded that his engine sounded okay and that he was not hurt. He also nodded that he thought his P-47 would make it to the coast. Austin then turned his formation on a course of 240 dgrees and headed for the coast;

'For the first two minutes, five Me 109s flew to our right and slightly above, but did not attack. There were seven of us. After five minutes on course, the receiver in "X53" apparently stopped working as the fighter drifted continuously to the left. We were at 6000 ft, about four miles north of Via Reggio, when I noticed his prop slow down and start windmilling. The ship slowed down noticeably, and a few seconds later Lt Ryan was seen to bail out. His 'chute opened at approximately 5500 ft and he drifted eastward. When last seen, he was at about 200 ft dropping into a wooded area between two hills. We did not circle him as we did not want to give his position away.'

A few weeks later, Lt Ryan was able to make his way through friendly lines and get back to the 86th FS.

MORE TO CORSICA

While the three operational Thunderbolt groups were escorting XII Bomber Command's 'mediums', two additional groups moved to Corsica with their new P-47s to finish conversion to the type. Both units had established an impressive combat record, and were old hands at the fighter-bomber role. The 86th FG moved to Porretto, in close proximity to Alto and Ghisonaccia on the Corsican east coast.

The 86th had been the second A-36 unit in the Mediterranean, and its pilots were extremely reluctant to give up their aeroplanes for new Thunderbolts, hoping instead for P-51 Mustangs. The 'Invaders' were very vocal about their disdain for transitioning to the P-47, and they excelled at creating derogatory nicknames for the Republic fighter. 'Old

Overbolts', 'Republic's Repulsive Fat Boy' and 'Flying Milk Bottle' were some of the less colourful sobriquets. One of their sharpest criticisms of the aeroplane was its high rate of fuel consumption. At normal power settings, the P-47 consumed a modest 90 to 130 gallons per hour. However, at the high power settings most often used in combat, in order to help cool the R-2800's massive cylinders, fuel consumption could jump as high as 315 gallons per hour at War Emergency Power! For pilots used to the relative fuel economy of the A-36's Allison V-1710 engine, this was a rude awakening. However, in the coming months, the 86th's pilots would turn these epithets into terms of endearment for the aeroplane that would bring many of them home, having absorbed damage that would have destroyed a lesser machine.

The 86th FG's association with the Thunderbolt got off to a rocky start. In the first month of operations with the P-47, the 526th and 527th FSs lost a total of 12 aircraft destroyed or damaged, the majority during transition training, although their first combat loss, Flt Off Douglas V Neale, was downed on his, and the unit's, second mission in the P-47.

The 527th was the group's first squadron to be cleared for combat missions, flying its initial sorties on 14 July when Lt Frank Myrick led a 12-ship mission to cut the rail and communication lines between Carpi and Suzzara. Myrick, who had been a police officer in San Diego prior to America's entry into World War 2, was an aggressive and well respected flight leader. Although he had flown the A-36 for most of his tour, Myrick quickly became adept at handling the Thunderbolt.

Despite the lousy weather, the 527th followed Myrick's lead and destroyed ten wagons, four vehicles and three gun positions on its first mission. Myrick's luck ran out a few days later while strafing flak batteries a few miles outside of Pisa. At extreme low altitude, his fighter, P-47D 42-26593, exploded while duelling with the 20 mm antiaircraft gun he was strafing. Described as 'brave, daring and sometimes reckless, Lt Myrick led the squadron on many excellent missions, and was liked and respected by his fellow pilots and crews'. The loss of an experienced flight leader like Myrick hit the 527th hard.

The 324th FG's transition to the Thunderbolt went more smoothly. The 316th FS arrived at Ghisonaccia on 18 July and turned in its war-weary P-40s for new P-47s. Several groundcrews from the 57th travelled down from Alto to help instruct their compatriots in the 324th on the P-47. The two units had operated together in North Africa, and the bond between personnel of both groups was apparent. The 316th was declared ready for its first mission in the new aeroplanes on 30 July, and the group flew its inaugural mission – a fighter sweep over Turin – with nothing significant to report. The 314th and 315th FSs followed suit on 1 and 2 August, flying similar sweeps over southern France and Genoa, respectively. Unknown to them at the time, the 314th's mission had

XII TAC maintenance was always performed in the field, regardless of the weather. Here, a 527th FS 'razorback' is undergoing a complete engine change (*Dave Hoover Collection*)

Lt Stan Hart and two other 314th FS pilots pose with the former's '36' somewhere in southern France. Hart's P-47D-25 is armed with a pair of 1000-lb GP bombs, which are more than likely intended for bridges in the Rhone River valley to cut off the retreating German 19th Army (*Author's Collection*)

signalled the start of a new phase of operations for the 324th FG over southern France. The group's participation in the Italian campaign was rapidly drawing to a close.

The following week saw a return to full time dive-bombing and strafing for most of the P-47 groups. Occasional escorts were still undertaken as needed, but the majority of missions flown over Italy were against rail and road targets. However, on 22 July, the 523rd FS was given a prime target to attack – the Luftwaffe's critically important airfield at Bergamo. A significant portion of Luftwaffe activity that XII TAC P-47s encountered during the summer of 1944 originated from Bergamo, and the 523rd jumped at the opportunity to hit the enemy at its home field.

523rd FS CO Lt Col William Nevitt led the maximum effort mission, splitting his squadron into two sections. Twelve aeroplanes would fly top cover in case any enemy aircraft had left the airfield, while the remainder would strafe the base at minimum altitude.

Nevitt called for the attacking flight to form three sections of four aeroplanes to strafe the airfield line-abreast, thus maximising the coverage of their 0.50-cals on one pass. The unit's operations report noted that 'the aircraft were at an altitude of no more than 25 ft as they strafed, and they were able to destroy two Macchi 202s, three Ju 88s and one Me 210 (actually an Me 410 of 2 *Staffel, Aufklarungsgruppe* 122). Most of the aircraft were in revetments and well camouflaged. Leaving the dispersal area, more than 30 tents in a wooded encampment were strafed, as were a few scattered buildings. In adition, three motor vehicles along the perimeter roads were destroyed'.

One of the 523rd's pilots, Capt Leonard Wiehrdt, 'was having a good time pumping holes in German aeroplanes and didn't notice the high-tension wire that loomed up ahead of him. He hit the cable at about 350 mph and made some awfully nasty dents and cuts in his own aeroplane. According to all the laws of average, Capt Wiehrdt is supposed to be smeared all over the landscape, but he finished the mission and flew the crippled aircraft home and landed safely'. Wiehrdt's piloting skill led him to become the commandant of the USAF Test Pilot School after the war. Unfortunately, he was killed in a Pilatus PC 6 crash in Laos while flying for *Air America* in 1972.

With five groups of P-47s on Corsica by 1 August, XII TAC was clearly on the move westward. The beginning of August saw a sharp increase in fighter-bomber sorties over southern France, lending further credence to the idea that the invasion was imminent. A Fifth Army directive to its subordinate divisions, acknowledging the shift of forces westward, attempted to assuage any fears that units in the field would be losing their air cover;

'XII TAC will, however, shortly be moved from the Italian theatre to support operations elsewhere. When that happens DAF will provide the

Groundcrewmen adjust the newly-installed M10 rocket launchers under the wings of '62'. These new weapons had mixed results, for although they provided the P-47 with devastating firepower, the rockets were often difficult to aim and impossible to control once they had left the tubes (*USAF World War 2 Collection*)

Lt Col Gil Wymond's P-47D 42-27910 *HUN HUNTER XIV*, armed with 500-lb bombs and rockets, escorts B-25s from Corsica on a low-level raid to northern Italy (*USAF World War 2 Collection*)

close support for both armies, and although DAF is being reinforced, resources available for that purpose will be less than heretofore. This must be accepted, but every effort will be made to meet the requirements of both armies. Priorities between armies as regards air support will be decided by HQ AAI.'

What this did not say was that 75 per cent of the tactical air assets needed to support Fifth Army's offensive operations would be pulled away for an extended period of time. Fighter-bomber units would be supporting the offensive in southern France, as would the sole tactical reconnaissance squadron (the 111th TRS, flying the F-6 Mustang reconnaissance variant of the P-51) in-theatre. The DAF was certainly a more than capable organisation, but its squadrons were busy enough supporting the Eighth Army, without having to also cover the US Fifth. Had the Luftwaffe been able to mount a serious air offensive in the late summer of 1944, things could have gone badly for Fifth Army.

The 57th FG's final mission of July introduced a new weapon to the Thunderbolt's repertoire. On the 65th FS's third and final mission of the day, unit CO Lt Col Gil Wymond had new M10 rocket tubes fitted to his P-47. These triple ten-foot tubes each fired a 40-lb rocket with the equivalent firepower of a 105 mm artillery round out to a range of 4600 yards, giving the Thunderbolt a significantly greater punch while remaining further away from the target. The late afternoon mission was another long-range foray into northeastern Italy to bomb the railway line between Poggio Rusco and San Felice. Four cuts were made along the tracks, with the final ones being done at the marshalling yard in San Felice.

Lt Col Wymond located a locomotive pulling 20 wagons and unleashed his rockets on it, blowing up the engine with one pull of the trigger. With a successful combat introduction of the new system, XII TAC requested more M10s for the fighter groups on Corsica for upcoming operations – later the following month, squadrons began carrying rocket projectiles. The final comment in the 65th's daily journal for July reads 'first rockets we have used, but hope we get more!'

AIRFIELD RAIDERS

As the invasion of southern France drew closer, the Twelfth Air Force sought to reduce the potential Luftwaffe threat as much as possible. While posing minimal danger to the invading ground forces, a massed Luftwaffe attack on the invasion fleet could be devastating. In order to prevent this, both XII Bomber Command and XII TAC targeted known Luftwaffe airfields in northern Italy and southern France, hoping to catch as many aeroplanes on the ground as possible.

The morning's mission on 2 August had the 85th FS headed back to northern Italy to continue attacks on Luftwaffe airfields. Crossing the Italian coast near La Spezia, where German antiaircraft batteries offered their usual welcome salute, the 'Skullmen' dropped their bombs on a bridge west of Bergamo, badly damaging the span. Now free from their encumbering loads, the formation turned towards the nearby airfield at treetop height. The squadron roared in and caught several German aeroplanes in the open, destroying many. Lt Vincent Millican, flying in the No 4 position in the lead flight, pulled up after his strafing pass and immediately had three large-calibre flak bursts explode beneath his aeroplane. From 4000 ft his aeroplane went into a spin, going through four complete turns before hitting the ground in a fireball.

Heading back to Serragia to rearm and refuel, the 85th left Bergamo's barracks and several other buildings burning, along with a Ju 88, a flak battery and a truck confirmed destroyed.

Following the loss of Lt Millican, a 59-mission veteran, the 85th's pilots were out for retribution. Launching as soon as the squadron's aeroplanes were refuelled and rearmed, they headed back north. Hitting several airfields, including Bergamo, the 'Skullmen' exacted revenge for their fallen comrade. The 85th positively destroyed eight Ju 88s, an SM.79, an SM.84 and a Me 410, probably destroyed another five Ju 88s, two SM.79s and another Me 410, and damaged five Ju 88s, 14 SM.79s, a single Ju 52/3m and an Fw 190, before heading home.

One of several He 111 night intruders that fell victim to P-47s during airfield strafing attacks (*Jackie Kaar*)

The next morning continued the 79th FG's attacks on Luftwaffe airfields in northern Italy with another two missions by the 85th. The unit claimed a Ju 87, a Do 217 and two unidentified transports destroyed, a pair of Ju 52/3ms as probables and seven Ju 88s, three Do 217s and a Ju 52/3m damaged. The day's second mission, however, saw Lt James Greene killed on his first combat mission when his aeroplane was hit by flak while diving on the target.

Although an obsolete design, the destruction and damage inflicted on the Do 217Ks of III./KG 100 probably had the greatest effect on the Luftwaffe's ability to attack the *Dragoon* invasion fleet. These twin-engined bombers were equipped to carry the Hs 293 radio-controlled glide

bomb, a weapon optimised for anti-shipping attacks. Although the unit's capability to launch attacks with the Hs 293 was severely curtailed by the 79th's attacks, a single III./KG 100 Do 217K was subsequently able to make a successful glide-bomb strike on the invasion fleet on the evening of D-Day, 15 August, sinking LST-282 with many of the 36th Division Artillery's 155 mm guns aboard.

By sundown on 4 August, the 79th had hit most of the known Luftwaffe bases in northwestern Italy, with the 87th FS even attacking Villa Franca airfield in southern France. The group wrought havoc on the enemy but lost three pilots killed in the process, vividly illustrating both the operational effectiveness and inherent dangers of low altitude strafing on German airfields.

The 86th FG joined in the airfield assault a week later, sending the 525th and 527th FSs to escort 33 B-26s of the 320th BG back to Bergamo, where they dropped 3783 20-lb fragmentation ('frag') bombs on the airfield. At a predetermined point, each squadron broke off in turn to strafe Bergamo before the bombers arrived. Instead of targeting aircraft on the field, the P-47 pilots pinpointed and silenced a number of flak positions to make the bomb run easier for the B-26s. After the mission, the 320th BG's deputy commander, and leader of the B-26 formation, Lt Col James Macia (of 'Doolittle Raid' fame) congratulated the Thunderbolt pilots on 'the best strafing job he'd ever seen'.

The 86th's squadrons were rapidly getting used to their new mounts, flying at least two missions per day in the lead-up to *Dragoon*. On 11 August the 527th sent an eight-ship mission to Marseilles to bomb a *Seetakt* surface search radar with 20-lb 'frag' clusters. Destroying this and other radars along the coast would delay German response times once the invasion fleet was sighted, giving the Allies the advantage of surprise.

As the squadron headed in toward the French coast, Lt James Whiting, leading 'White' flight, saw that deteriorating cloud conditions might affect the mission's progress;

'We approached the target to our north/northeast. The haze was very bad, with overcast some 500 ft thick at 10,000 ft – this began in layers from about five miles inland. "Red" flight approached the overcast and

The 85th FS was extensively engaged supporting the advancing Seventh Army during Operation *Dragoon*. This squadron aeroplane suffered a collapsed landing gear while taxiing on 22 September 1944 at Bron airfield, near Lyon, France (*Dave Hoover Collection*)

Lt Col George Lee's P-47D 42-28604 *DORA PAT III* escorts B-26s of the 320th BG over northern Italy on one of the many bridge and rail interdiction runs flown against targets in the Po River valley in 1944 (*Fred Schmidt via M Adamic*)

flew into it. Although my flight was staying close to me, when I went under the overcast my wingman, Lt Arnold Landan, went over it. The rest of my element followed me under. I did not see Lt Landan again.'

Being an inexperienced pilot on his first combat mission, Landan's confidence in his instrument flying may have been the reason why he chose to go above the clouds instead of through them. Unfortunately, this separated him from his flight – a fatal mistake. Whiting continues;

'I called him and told him to get into position, but heard no answer from him. "Red" flight proceeded to make a large 360-degree turn while I followed. As I passed over the town of Marseille, accurate 88 mm flak started breaking off my right wing. "Red" flight had, by this time, completed 270 degrees of its turn and was over some small islands. Flak started breaking around the P-47s. I was busy doing evasive action and watching the rest of my flight, and did not observe "Red" flight too closely. As "Red" flight went into its dive, I noticed a P-47 spinning down, pouring out black smoke. It was directly under the flak from the islands. I went into my bombing dive and broke right so as to turn away from where I had seen the P-47 spinning in, and I saw a large spot on the water burning, sending up a thick column of black smoke. This was approximately six miles south of Marseille.'

Good hits were obtained on the radar and its associated equipment, temporarily blinding German early warning in that sector.

It was assumed that flak from the islands off Marseille had hit Landan's P-47, but Luftwaffe historian Nick Beale has confirmed that the fighter was actually shot down by Oberfeldwebel Eduard Isken, a 41-kill *Experte* from the only Luftwaffe fighter unit in the vicinity, 2./JGr. 200. Seeing a lone P-47 above the clouds, Isken's flight of six Bf 109s pounced on the inexperienced Landan and shot him down.

As D-Day drew closer, XII TAC's Thunderbolts continued to hit airfields and coastal defences from Toulon to northern Italy. On the 13th, the 57th FG mounted another group effort of 36 aeroplanes to hit Bergamo for the fourth time in a week. Although battered and cratered, the base continued to be a hub of Luftwaffe activity in the Mediterranean, and the threat of Ju 88s or Do 217s flying from there in number against the invasion fleet was too great to let rebuild.

The 65th led the attack, and its pilots claimed the only aeroplanes on the airfield – two Ju 88s and a single He 111 – damaged, but these may have already been rendered unflyable by earlier attacks. The 64th and 66th FSs dove down to strafe, but pilots noted that 'due to the depleted number of the once invincible Luftwaffe, pickings were few'.

The 324th FG flew a two-squadron mission to Les Chanoines airfield in the late evening. The 316th FS was the first to reach the aerodrome at 1950 hrs, and its flight of 12 P-47s caught several aeroplanes in the open in the fading daylight. Coming in at almost zero altitude, the 'Hell's Belles' strafed a number of aircraft, Lt James Huggins setting a Bf 110 on fire and damaging a Ju 88, while Lt George Potts did the same with an He 111 and a second Ju 88. Lt Edwin Harley also claimed an He 111 'flamer'. Turning the show over to the 314th, the latter added five more aircraft damaged (four Ju 88s and a Bf 110) and then shot up a hangar and several buildings, as well as destroying the airfield's large steel water tower, before heading back to Corsica.

While the enemy's airfields had been mercilessly hammered, his coastal defences had been left relatively untouched by the marauding Thunderbolts of XII TAC. Although aware that they would be expected to make a maximum effort, and put up every flyable airframe to cover the invasion force, some squadrons elected to fly one mission on the 14th. The 315th FS loaded its P-47s up with 'frag' clusters and went after radar sites along the French coast, destroying two *Freyas* and damaging a *Wurzburg*, significantly reducing the German early warning capabilities.

The rest of the day was filled with briefings on tactical procedures and what to expect over the beachhead in the coming days. One of the key organisations intended to deconflict the airspace over the beachhead was the Fighter Bomber Direction Center aboard the Amphibious Force Command Ship USS *Catoctin* (AGC-5). While two other vessels would act as Fighter Direction Centers, orchestrating the air defence for the invasion fleet, controllers of the 2nd Air Combat Control Squadron (Amphibious) (ACCS(A)) aboard *Catoctin* would be responsible for directing all inbound P-47 flights from Corsica. These controllers would be briefed on all incoming missions, and they would tell the units whether to hit their primary or alternate targets prior to the squadrons making landfall.

In addition to monitoring all fighter-bomber traffic over the beachhead, the Joint Operations Room on *Catoctin* would receive fighter-bomber and tactical reconnaissance mission requests from units ashore. From there, liaison officers of VI Corps, Seventh Army and XII TAC would be able to set a priority level for the mission and then pass it onto the controllers of the 2nd ACCS(A), using the callsign 'Boxcar'. Inbound P-47 squadrons would check in with 'Boxcar' and authenticate their mission target number. If 'Boxcar' had a higher priority target, the controller would then re-task the Thunderbolts with the new mission. On several occasions on D-Day through to D+4, friendly ground forces had already advanced past pre-planned fighter-bomber targets, resulting in P-47 squadrons being hastily re-tasked with missions ahead of the bomb line.

Due to the increasing distances XII TAC Thunderbolts had to fly from Corsica, and the rapid advance of friendly ground forces, by D+3 all fighter-bomber missions over the beachhead were changed to armed reconnaissance following the removal of bombs from wing racks. This allowed the P-47 pilots to work closer to friendly forces without fear of blast or fragmentation fratricide, but it stymied their effectiveness when called on to destroy a bridge or railway line.

D-DAY

With the sheer numbers of aeroplanes in the skies over the Cote d'Azur, all five P-47 groups chose to fly greater mission numbers with fewer sorties so as to provide the best coverage over the beachhead on D-Day. Starting well before dawn, flights of four P-47s took off from airfields across Corsica and joined the massive air armada headed northwest to France. As the first flights made landfall, low-lying haze obscured many of their intended targets, and a layered overcast between 2000 ft and 8000 ft made locating and identifying targets extremely difficult, but by 0730 hrs it had started to clear.

After scrubbing two scheduled missions due to lack of target identification, the 324th FG was one of the first groups to hit its targets, with the 315th FS taking off for its first fighter-bomber mission at 0445 hrs. The 314th bombed a pair of coastal guns at 0745 hrs, putting six bombs on target and two nearby. The 316th, originally intending to bomb a battery of four 150 mm guns, was diverted to its secondary target by 'Boxcar', as weather was still a factor over the primary target.

The 79th began its day when the first aeroplanes took off at 0425 hrs to patrol over the invasion beachhead. Its operations report noted;

'Over the entire field, spotted green and red lights from aeroplane wingtips and the deep purple colour from the exhaust tubes made a beautiful sight as the crew chiefs preflighted 100 P-47s around the field. Through the long lasting night and busy day, gallons of coffee were dispensed to keep the men from falling asleep on their feet, but inspiration from the masses of aircraft, Army, Navy and Allied, steadily droning overhead hundreds at a time kept them going at a furious clip, and each successful landing or bits of news on our troops' forward advance was greeted by loud cheers and gleeful smiles.'

The 87th FS lost one pilot late in the day while strafing west of Nice. The formation had made two passes over a fleeing motor transport column, destroying a number of trucks, when Lt James Williams' P-47 was hit by fire from the column. According to his flight leader, Lt Herbert Hanson, Williams' aeroplane looked undamaged, but as the flight headed out to sea, it lost altitude and bellied in offshore. No attempt was made by Lt Williams to get out of the aeroplane, and it sank after floating for about ten seconds on the surface.

The Twelfth Air Force's P-47 squadrons averaged nine complete missions on D-Day, when normally scheduled for only two per day. Quickly shifting between fighter-bomber, bomber escort and armed reconnaissance roles, XII TAC's Thunderbolts maintained a constant umbrella over the beachhead, destroying targets of opportunity when they arose and contributing significantly to the successes of the day.

The Luftwaffe did make one showing. A four-ship patrol from the 65th FS, having completed its patrol over the beachhead just before 2100 hrs, was heading back to Corsica when the 2nd ACCS(A) controller 'Baby' called that there was an unidentified aircraft inbound toward the invasion fleet. In actuality, there were two enemy aircraft, a Ju 88 and an Hs 293-armed Do 217. The 65th FS Thunderbolts, along with 50 other aircraft, were already halfway back to Corsica when the call came over the net. Risking a fuel-critical situation if they turned back, all of the outbound aircraft continued to head home. As previously noted in this chapter, the enemy aeroplanes attacked the beachhead, with the Ju 88 dropping bombs inland and the Do 215 sinking LST-282 with the war's last successful anti-shipping launch of an Hs 293.

By the end of D-Day, Allied forces had pushed more than five miles inland, and they continued to make similar gains in the days to follow. As VI Corps spearheaded Seventh Army's drive northward, XII TAC quickly became its eyes in the sky, locating troop concentrations, vehicles and routes along which the German Army Group G was in full retreat. After expending their ordnance, Thunderbolts became valued reconnaissance platforms, calling in targets of opportunity to higher

Lt Col George Lee inspecting the K-25 camera installed in the left pylon of his P-47 prior to a mission. Lee served as the deputy commander of the 86th FG until February 1945, when he was promoted to become the group's CO (*USAF World War 2 Collection*)

headquarters, who then added them to the priority target list for P-47s just arriving from Corsica. With only one tactical reconnaissance squadron assigned to XII TAC, and Thunderbolt units conducting armed reconnaissance, it was only a matter of time before the K-25 pylon camera field modification began seeing wider use in order to capture battlefield imagery.

Although Thunderbolts had carried M17 500-lb incendiaries prior to the invasion, a new type of fire bomb was also introduced during the opening days of the campaign. By D+3, P-47s were no longer carrying bombs, so three auxiliary fuel tanks became the standard load. In order to increase their firepower, the lead aeroplane would drop his tanks on the target and his wingman would then strafe them, setting them ablaze. Lt James 'Mac' McPherson of the 527th was one of the first to try this new technique out on the 17th, when he dropped the tanks on a 40-wagon train of oil tankers and boxcars, setting a number of them ablaze.

The mission's climax, however, came when flight leader Lt Harry Caldwell made his second strafing pass on the train. His 0.50-cal rounds found their mark when they hit a boxcar loaded with ammunition, and the resulting explosion threw debris 2500 ft into the air, much of which hit Caldwell's P-47. Forced to bail out over enemy territory, he had rejoined the 527th within a week.

This improvised fire bomb proved very effective, and as a result groundcrews adjusted their P-47s' ammunition loads to make greater use of tracer or Armour-Piercing Incendiary rounds, which could ignite the discarded tanks. Groundcrew innovation also saw the tanks adapted through the fitting of impact fuses, turning them into true fire bombs.

The 526th had an equally eventful day on 19 August, flying four missions over the invasion front. As Army Group G retreated, the road network leading north was clogged with German vehicles of all types that were left with nowhere to run when the 526th's Thunderbolts rolled in with guns blazing. On the last mission of the day, Lt Bert Benear single-handedly took on three WGr.21 rocket-armed Bf 109s of JGr. 200 that had been attacking French Resistance positions near Vallon Pont d'Arc. Downing one and damaging another, he then took numerous hits to his own machine and was forced to disengage and nurse his damaged aeroplane home.

NEW AIRFIELDS

Following Seventh Army's lightning advance, the necessity for XII TAC to move to the invasion front became apparent. The 27th, 79th and 324th FGs were given movement orders on 18 August, and within 48 hours, advanced parties for all three groups were preparing the airfields at Le Luc and San Raphael, on the continent.

The 27th FG claimed the honour of flying XII TAC's first combat mission from French soil when it departed Le Luc at 0900 hrs on 20 August to escort a flight of B-25s coming in from Corsica. By that evening, two squadrons of the 324th had their aeroplanes based at Le Luc, opposite the 27th FG. Two days later, the 79th moved to St Raphael airfield. The operational pace did not slow much as each squadron continued to fly four interdiction missions per day, knocking out road bridges and strafing retreating German forces.

While the Thunderbolts were flying continuous missions in support of the advance, the distance between airfield and frontline continued to grow. Five days after moving in to Le Luc, the 27th FG moved north to Salon in an effort to catch up with Seventh Army. The 324th FG's 314th FS arrived at Le Luc on the 29th, but it was packing to head to a new airfield just two days later. 29 August also saw Lt William Littlewood of the 316th score the 324th FG's last kill of the month when he downed Oberfeldwebel Beller's Bf 109 'Yellow 1' from *Sonderstaffel* 'Kaatsch'.

The 57th and 86th FGs continued to fly from Corsica, and on the 29th the 527th FS received two replacement aeroplanes, one of them a brand new P-47D-28 fitted with a Curtiss Electric C542S 'paddle-blade' propeller and a new electric bomb release system. With the aircraft's improved performance and stunning rate of climb, the pilots of the 527th anxiously waited to see who would claim it as their assigned machine.

Lt Gen Alexander Patch's Seventh Army solidified its front on 5 September, linking up with Gen Patton's Third Army on its left flank. The Allied front was now a continuous line from the Mediterranean coast to the North Sea, pushing eastward. Thunderbolt squadrons had seen some of their heaviest losses during July and August, primarily due to the nature of the missions flown, and as Allied armies advanced towards final victory, the number of P-47 pilots killed would continue to climb.

As the campaign in France pressed north and east towards Germany, XII TAC remained under the control of the 1st Tactical Air Force (Provisional) and continued to provide air support and battlefield interdiction for the advancing Seventh Army. 1st TACAF was a conglomeration of XII TAC, the Free French 1st Air Corps and elements of the US Ninth Air Force.

And while the other groups of XII TAC would rotate back and forth between Italy and France for the rest of 1944, the 324th FG would remain at the forefront of 1st TACAF's movements and would not see Italian soil again.

San Raphael airfield, in France, was home to the 79th FG for a few short weeks in late August and early September 1944. As the Allied advance pushed northwards, however, it was soon out of range of the frontlines, forcing the 79th to move to Valence for the rest of the month, before the group returned to Italy (*Dave Hoover Collection*)

It was not always all business. Here, from left to right, Lts Patteson, Harley, Wilbur and Richmond of the 316th FS are seen during a lighter moment at Dole-Tavaux, in southern France (*Doug Patteson*)

RAIN, MUD AND MOUNTAINS

Once XII TAC was firmly established in southern France and supporting Seventh Army as it advanced northwards, the 57th and 86th FGs turned their mission focus back to Italy. Many in the 57th questioned why they were not included among those groups that continued on in France, since they had been in the vanguard of both the Ninth and Twelfth Air Forces from North Africa through to their arrival on

Corsica. Instead, the 57th remained on the island with the 86th, both groups being reassigned to the British DAF. Returning to Po valley missions in northern Italy, pilots quickly realised that a move would be in order shortly, as Thunderbolts from both units often had to 'gas up' at Grosseto en route back to Corsica.

Missions continued to be flown from Corsica in early September, however, P-47s once again targeting the German 14th Army's supply network. 2 September was a particularly successful day for the 65th FS, which flew three missions to northern Italy and added to the group's sunken shipping tonnage. The day's second mission began as a four-ship armed reconnaissance, but mechanical trouble forced one aeroplane to turn back. Maj Hunziker and Lts Harry Meyd and Max Floerke continued on to reconnoitre Genoa harbour, finding a number of ripe targets. The three sighted, and attacked, a vessel 'the size of a Liberty ship' that was being towed out of its slip by a tug. Hunziker and Meyd targeted the larger vessel, dropping three 500-lb bombs directly on it and strafing as they passed, while Floerke hit the tug, leaving it burning.

Twenty-four hours earlier, the final P-47 unit in Italy was certified operational after converting from the P-39 Airacobra. The 350th FG had arrived in England in 1942, where it had briefly flown P-39s before joining the Twelfth Air Force in North Africa. Having seen action here and in Italy, the 350th was flying maritime patrols in P-39Qs by August 1944, with detachments in several locations along the western Italian coast. With the reduction of the Axis maritime threat in the MTO, the Twelfth Air Force began re-equipping the 350th with P-47s.

The 350th's squadrons (345th, 346th and 347th FSs) flew their first P-47 combat missions the same day they were declared operational, bombing two occupied towns north of the Po in support of Italian

Lt Joseph Angelone's *"TOOTS/LIL' ABNER"* (a P-47D-26) was destroyed in a takeoff accident at Grosseto on 6 October 1944 which the pilot walked away from with barely a scratch (*Joseph Angelone collection via 57thfighter group.com/Mark O'Boyle*)

The 65th FS attacked Genoa harbour on 2 September and hit this large cargo vessel amidships with three 500-lb bombs, leaving it burning (*USAF World War 2 Collection*)

partisans. As the 350th became familiar with the combat handling and ordnance delivery characteristics of the P-47, its record of vehicles, trains and enemy materiel destroyed began to increase rapidly. Unlike the remaining five Thunderbolt groups in the MTO, the 350th did not ease into the aircraft by flying bomber escort missions, but immediately began carrying out low-level CAS and interdiction sorties over the Apennines.

On 12 September, Fifth and Eighth Armies commenced Operation *Olive* – the combined assault on 'Gothic Line' defences in the Apennine Mountains, the last hurdle before the Po River valley. Twelfth Air Force was to provide air cover for the advancing armies, and the initial air attacks were designed to destroy dug-in Axis positions south of the Po.

As Twelfth Air Force bombers took off from Corsica and Sardinia en route to the Po River valley, the 86th FG swept into the target area on an 'flak delousing' mission. This was the most dangerous type of operation flown by the Twelfth's P-47s, with missions like this suffering the highest loss rates. The tactic was to fly down the valley ahead of the bomber formation and get the antiaircraft guns to shoot at you. Once the batteries began firing at the P-47s, they would be attacked with 500-lb bombs and machine gun fire. All three units duelled with several gun positions along the valley, silencing several with bombs and 0.50-cal fire.

On one firing pass, Lt Bill Goslin's aeroplane, nicknamed *VIV'S BABY SHOES* after his daughter Vivian, took 20 mm flak hits that severed an oil line. Goslin turned for the coast, and as his engine began to run roughly he ditched in the Ligurian Sea. Covered in oil but otherwise alright, Goslin was quickly picked up by an RAF Air-Sea Rescue boat and returned to the 527th by nightfall.

On the afternoon of 16 September, 346th FS CO Maj Andrew Schindler led a 12-ship attack on an ammunition factory just north of the 'Gothic line'. The factory had continued to supply German units despite previous attacks, and the 346th was given the job of destroying it. Some 18 bombs fell on the factory, causing immense secondary explosions and massive fires in and around the area. With its primary target destroyed, the 346th continued north to intercept trains coming south to reinforce the German 10th Army on the Adriatic coast. One train loaded with tanks, halftracks and other vehicles was found and attacked, leaving the locomotive smoking and 19 wagons destroyed or severely damaged.

While the Thunderbolts were wreaking havoc on the enemy's air defences and supply routes, Fifth and Eighth Armies continued to push northwards. Indeed, the 91st Division seized the Il Giogo pass and the 85th captured Monte Altuzzo by the 18th, forcing the German 1st *Fallschirmjäger* division to retreat or be outflanked. This in turn allowed Fifth Army to attain its second objective – the capture of the Futa Pass – on the 22nd. During the advance, XXII TAC had maintained a regular P-47 presence overhead, despite increasingly poor weather conditions.

On the 346th's fourth mission of the day on 29 September, Maj Schindler engaged and shot down the 350th FG's first enemy aircraft since becoming operational with the P-47. Pulling up from his bomb run, Schindler sighted a lone Fw 190 at a height of just 200 ft, several miles away. Diving to catch up with the Focke-Wulf, Schindler closed to within 500 yards before opening up on it. The Fw 190 banked sharply and tried to evade, but Schindler, now just 300 yards away, adjusted his

Lt Bill Goslin's personal mount, P-47D 42-28132 *VIV'S BABY SHOES*, was named for his daughter Vivian and served faithfully until damaged on an anti-flak mission in the Po River valley on 12 September (*Dave Hoover Collection*)

Lt Goslin flew his damaged P-47 back to the Ligurian coast, where he was forced to ditch in the Ligurian Sea. He was picked up by this RAF Air-Sea Rescue launch, and he is seen here pointing to the American star marking that denoted his safe rescue (*Dave Hoover Collection*)

Holding up his oil-soaked flight suit next to a member of the RAF launch crew displaying his emergency dinghy, Bill Goslin had returned to the 527th just hours after ditching (*Dave Hoover Collection*)

One of the outstandingly effective new weapons developed in the autumn of 1944 was the 110-gallon napalm tank. P-47s had been using partially empty external fuel tanks as incendiary bombs in southern France, but the new 'Fuel Tank Incendiary' gave a much better dispersal of the flame agent. Here, a flight of four 65th FS aeroplanes demonstrates a level bombing attack with the new weapon on Corsica (*USAF World War 2 Collection*)

aim accordingly. As his rounds found their mark, the Focke-Wulf's canopy flew off and the pilot bailed out.

NEW DEVELOPMENTS

As October began, so did the rainy season. While the infantry fought bitterly for every yard of ground in the Apennines, their air support remained grounded for a significant portion of the month. When the rains did let up, bomb-laden aeroplanes were prevented from taxiing by a sea of mud. In conjunction with the offensive, experienced pilots began rotating up to the frontlines to join 'Rover Joe' teams to more effectively talk P-47s onto their targets.

October saw the introduction of several innovations in both weapons and equipment. The 527th's 3 October morning mission marked the first use of new 110-gallon incendiary tanks. The new napalm tanks were 'filled with gasoline and a gelatinous substance and fused with small grenades which ignite on impact', and were first used to attack an enemy command post and artillery position just north of the bomb line.

As Lt John Boone led the flight inbound to the target, his P-47 was hit by flak. He maintained control of his aeroplane and initiated the attack, dropping his napalm on target, despite an engine fire. Pulling up to roughly 3000 ft, Boone initially intended to bail out, but decided he could make it back to friendly territory and elected to stay with his stricken fighter. The P-47 steadily lost altitude until, according to Lt John Robinson, at about 1000 ft Boone's right wing dropped and the fighter 'dived into a hillside and exploded'.

The remainder of the flight reported 'a dazzling display with flames and smoke covering a large area', but the pilots' initial assessment of the new napalm tanks was not very enthusiastic. They were difficult to drop effectively because the tanks tumbled once released, and in order to get the best target effect, the pilot had to fly at a much lower altitude, where he was more vulnerable to flak. The tanks did the job, however, and quickly became an invaluable weapon in the mountainous terrain.

Along with napalm, the M10 4.5-in rocket system began arriving in-theatre in greater numbers. During the first week of October, when the 66th FS did not fly at all, six of its aeroplanes were fitted with the new triple rocket tubes. The 27th and 350th FGs also began receiving rockets by late October, greatly enhancing their P-47s' combat capability.

Aside from the new weapons, 16 October saw the first G-3A G-suits arrive in-theatre. Early examples had originally been issued to Eighth Air Force groups in the ETO for air-to-air manoeuvring in order to prevent pilots from blacking out during high-G manoeuvres. The benefits of such equipment for fighter-bomber pilots performing high-G pullout manoeuvres over their targets was quickly realised, and the initial issue of the new garment

Along with napalm tanks, autumn 1944 saw the new M10 rocket tube system added to the Thunderbolt's arsenal. Although the weapon met with mixed results in the frontline, the ability to expend the equivalent weight of explosives as an entire six-gun 105 mm artillery battery in a single pass was an undeniable boost to the Thunderbolt's flexibility (*USAF World War 2 Collection*)

'Fighting Cocks'' armourer PFC Samuel Sanchez stands ready to load an M9 4.5-in rocket projectile into an M10 tube fitted to squadron aeroplane '46' (*USAF World War 2 Collection*)

to Thunderbolt units came surprisingly fast, although not all units were completely equipped until after 1 January 1945.

RENEWED OFFENSIVE

As Fifth Army gathered its strength for another push towards Bologna, MAAF HQ devised a new plan, codenamed Operation *Pancake*, whose object was the destruction of enemy supplies and equipment in the Bologna area. As the name implied, MAAF's intent was to bomb Bologna and the surrounding region 'flat'. Beginning on 10 October, the operation met with mixed results. Fighter-bomber flights were curtailed for the first day, but on the 11th they came out in force, working in conjunction with 'Rover Joe' controllers to hit targets just ahead of the bomb line.

Over the next two days the 350th FG, relatively new to CAS, flew 18 missions per day supporting the advance, its pilots giving 'very close support to Fifth Army's troops' and being commended for their skill. The 350th had some welcome reinforcements arrive in the middle of the month with the addition of the 1st Brazilian Fighter Squadron (BFS), which the group absorbed as its fourth squadron.

The 27th FG, freshly back from France, flew an equal number of missions in support of the offensive. On 20 October, the 522nd attacked the railway lines between Bologna and Ferrara, catching a diesel engine pulling 20 wagons of mixed types in the open. 'Red' flight, led by Lt William Kropf, dove on the train, hitting the engine and cutting the rails in front of it in two places. It then strafed the train while 'White' flight provided high cover. When 'Red' flight pulled up, 'White' flight expended its bombs, after which the formation climbed for altitude and turned for home.

Lt Bob Hoseler of the 522nd FS stands on the wing of his assigned aeroplane, P-47D 42-26444 *Candie Jr.*, in September 1944 (*1Sgt Mark Barry*)

One of the critical maintenance tasks with any fighter aircraft was the proper boresighting of the aeroplane's weapons. Making sure the 0.50-cal machine guns were aligned with the gunsight and set to converge at a point in space (usually around 300 yards) ahead of the aeroplane that would yield the greatest weight of fire on the target was critical to combat performance (*1Sgt Mark Barry*)

Lt Hoseler poses with his crew chief, SSgt Desjardins (*1Sgt Mark Barry*)

As they egressed the area, the flight was targeted by accurate 40 mm flak, some of which hit the engine in the P-47 of squadron CO, Capt Robert Fromm. Lt Bernard Hartman, flying on his wing, pulled in close to see if his commander was okay. 'He put the aeroplane in a dive and then without calling bailed out of its right side at approximately 9060 ft. He appeared to have cleared the P-47 without trouble. I lost sight of him as he fell, and could not spot his 'chute'. Fromm's parachute never opened.

Throughout the week the weather remained flyable, although at times only marginally so. By late morning missions were usually possible, but it was clear that the weather would be a decisive factor in determining *Pancake's* success. Several of the week's missions were delayed until conditions were clear enough to takeoff. While all of the pilots were trained to fly on instruments, it was essential that they visually acquired their targets before attacking them, and taking off as a formation and flying into poor weather conditions was often a recipe for disaster.

October's miserable weather allowed an average of only 14 flying days during the month. When able to support Fifth Army's advance, or attacking rail or communication targets north of the Po, the P-47 remained the weapon of choice, as its accuracy was unequalled. CAS missions focused on troop concentrations, gun emplacements and storage depots, particularly along Highway 65 – Fifth Army's main axis of advance. Interdiction missions continued too, ranging from the Po valley just north of the bomb line up to Lake Maggiore, on the Swiss border.

Despite the intense efforts of the 'Thunderbombers' over Fifth Army's advance, by 26 October the offensive had stalled. Several factors were blamed, but the underlying reason was simply that the Italian theatre had become of secondary importance to France. Fifth Army's divisions gave their all, fighting over incredibly difficult terrain against a well trained and dug-in enemy while facing shortages in both replacements and ammunition. In the 88th Division, troop strength had dropped to lower than 60 per cent despite making the greatest advance toward Bologna. As October came to a close, Fifth Army consolidated its gains and dug in defensive positions for the winter.

CONTINUING *STRANGLE*

Fifth Army's failure to decisively break through the German lines and capture Bologna by no means reduced the number of missions flown by

XXII TAC's Thunderbolts. Grosseto, where the 86th and 57th now flew from, was almost completely flooded out by 2 November when a dike north of the town overflowed due to the weeks of continuous rain. The pilots' quarters for both groups were completely deluged, with the first floors of each building now containing at least four feet of water.

The 86th had moved most of its personnel up to Pisa, but the flood that inundated Grosseto quickly had air- and groundcrews from the 527th FS heading north to join their comrades. The 57th soldiered on at Grosseto, the group resuming missions just in time for Operation *Bingo* – the MAAF's offensive against infrastructure around the Brenner Pass. While the Twelfth's medium bombers and the Fifteenth's heavy bombers blanketed the Brenner Pass with high explosives, the 66th FS took 16 aeroplanes to bomb the transformer station at Trento in support of the operation. Direct hits on the station created 'large blue-coloured explosions' from the detonation of the transformer equipment.

Missions were continuous on the 6th and 7th for all four groups in support of *Bingo*. The weather had held for the most part, but the forecast for the remainder of the week looked bleak. The 525th FS flew three napalm strikes on the 6th out of the five missions it completed, and four more on the 7th, all in northeastern Italy. One mission, led by Lt William Curtin, almost ended in disaster when one of his napalm tanks hung up on its rack, refusing to drop. While his flight executed their attack with precision, inundating the target area with flame, Curtin could not eject the hung tank. Returning to Pisa, he set his aeroplane down as gently as possible, but jarred the tank loose on touchdown. The tank separated from the aeroplane and detonated, spreading flames several hundred yards down the runway. Miraculously, both Lt Curtin and his aeroplane escaped unscathed!

After two days of stand down due to the rain, the 525th again took to the skies on 10 November, this time heading for Villafranca airfield north of Verona, loaded with 500-lb bombs. Lt F C Brinley, flying his P-47 *Love n' Stuff*, led the seven-ship mission, and on the first pass several bombs exploded close to a Ju 88 and two Bf 109s, but no aircraft were destroyed. Brinley led the formation around again, and despite intense flak the P-47s strafed the airfield, being credited with four confirmed destroyed (a Ju 88 and three Bf 109s) and a probable. Lt Walter Reiber accounted for the three confirmed Messerschmitts. As the pilots pulled up and headed back to Pisa, they discovered that five of their seven fighters had been holed by flak to varying degrees, but all returned safely.

Only half of the remaining days in November were deemed suitable for flying due to weather. With the lines mostly stable, Thunderbolt pilots were free to hunt locomotives and motor transport far behind enemy lines. As the pickings grew slimmer in the west, XXII TAC began assigning targets further east, both to support Eighth Army and the DAF and as a continuation of Operation *Bingo*. The 57th's squadrons kept up a continuous presence in northeastern Italy through the first two weeks of December, making the movement of any rail transport exceedingly difficult during the day.

At roughly 1030 hrs on 9 December, a 66th FS flight caught a train loaded with motor transport headed south to resupply the German 10th Army near Vicenza. Following their flight leader, the P-47 pilots initiated a strafing pass on the train, showing good hits and damaging a number of wagons. German machine gunners aboard the train were extremely accurate, however. As Lt Charles Dehmer pulled up from his pass, white smoke began to pour from his engine and supercharger. Several calls for him to bail out met with no response, and at an altitude of about 500 ft his aeroplane rolled over and plunged into the ground.

As the flight began to form back up, Capt Thomas Callan radioed the rest of the flight that he too had been hit and his oil pressure had dropped to zero. He attempted to climb and head east to ditch in the Adriatic, but as the rest of the flight caught up with him, it was clear he was going to have to bail out. Callan rolled his stricken aeroplane over and fell out of the cockpit, pulling the ripcord of his parachute once he was clear of the fighter's tail. He made it safely to the ground, but was captured shortly after by German forces.

The 66th's ordeal was not yet over. The day's second mission – an armed reconnaissance in the same vicinity that Dehmer and Callan went down – caught enemy trucks on a road. On his strafing pass, Lt Robert Lown 'mushed' into some trees and his aeroplane exploded. An hour later, and only a few miles east, a fourth 'Exterminators'' aeroplane went down. Lt Wayne Dodds managed to belly his P-47 into the Venetian lagoon in about three feet of water after a successful bombing run. Of the four pilots lost that day, he would be the only one to return to the unit, although it would take him a full month to do so. The unit lost Lt Eugene Smith the following afternoon, and in an eerie twist of fate, five brand new pilots were assigned to the 66th FS later that same day.

A SURPRISE OFFENSIVE

The morning of 26 December was a rude awakening for Fifth Army. With Christmas the previous night and the parlous state of German logistics, no one expected that the enemy would be capable of launching an offensive in the bitter cold, having been denied meaningful quantities of ammunition and gasoline for months. Yet in the early morning hours of the 26th, a combined German and Italian force of eight infantry battalions, supported by artillery, but little else, attacked across the 'Gothic line' into positions held by the fairly inexperienced African-American 92nd Infantry Division. The 'Buffalo Soldiers' had

Fully loaded with rockets and napalm, these 1st BFS P-47Ds sit lined up at Pisa awaiting their next mission over the Po River valley (*Cesar Maximiano Campiani*)

moved into positions along the Serchio River in early November and had conducted extensive patrolling in the area, but had not yet met the enemy as a division. The 366th Infantry Regiment was initially overwhelmed, but it was soon able to regroup and fought to delay the enemy onslaught as best it could.

Due to the failure of the division commander to communicate the severity of the situation to higher HQ, XXII TAC's Thunderbolts were never retasked with flying CAS

for the beleaguered defenders on the 26th. Instead, fighters from all four groups flew regularly scheduled missions against various rail and communications targets in northern Italy, rather than responding to the Axis breakthrough. On one of those missions, the 346th FS attacked Lonate/Pozzola airfield and claimed 12 SM.82 and four Ju 88 bombers destroyed without a shot being fired at them! By the time the severity of the breakthrough was known at XXII TAC, little could be done by air, so the majority of the following day's missions were retasked to provide CAS for the counterattack.

The frontlines had stabilised by the 27th, and any Axis troops caught in the open quickly became targets for 'frag' clusters, napalm and 0.50-cal machine guns. The enemy units had no armoured support and no fuel for motor transport, leaving them little choice but to withdraw on foot under the cover of darkness. By midday on the 30th, the frontlines had returned to roughly how they had appeared on Christmas Day.

The 1st BFS was busy on 31 December 1944, hitting a number of targets in northern Italy. Here, an ammunition storage shed near Trento is captured in a still frame from a 1st BFS Gun Sight Aiming Point camera during a strafing run (*Cesar Maximiano Campiani*)

Although the year was coming to a close, the operational pace continued as long as the weather held out. The 1st BFS celebrated two full months of combat operations from Pisa by flying three missions on 31 December. First off was an eight-ship flight from Pisa at 0755 hrs to dive-bomb the marshalling yards at Trento, in northern Italy. The flight was met by intense flak between Ostiglia and Melara as they egressed from the target area, but the damage had by then been done. Sixteen 500-lb bombs were dropped precisely on the marshalling yards, cutting the tracks in a number of places. On their way out, the pilots strafed any rolling stock that they could see, destroying eight wagons and damaging ten others.

An hour later, as the second flight was already airborne on a follow-up raid to Trento, weather moved in and forced it to hit the alternate target – an ammunition dump near Genoa. Thirteen bombs fell directly on the target area, destroying six storage sheds with spectacular results. Several vehicles near to the dump and in the immediate surrounding area were also strafed, two of them yielding huge secondary explosions. As the flight turned for Pisa, it caught a locomotive and roughly 100 wagons at Novoligure, holing the engine's boiler and damaging several wagons.

Tenente Coronel Nero Moura was CO of the 1st BFS in 1944-45 (*Cesar Maximiano Campiani*)

1944 had been a productive year for the Twelfth Air Force, taking a high altitude interceptor and adapting it for low-level air-to-ground work. The P-47 had evolved along with the tactics its pilots employed to maximise its strengths. Better bomb-release systems, improved visibility from the cockpit, uprated engines and more efficient propellers made the latest P-47D-28s reaching XII and XXII TAC a far cry from those early D-models flown just a few months before. As the New Year turned, XXII TAC's Thunderbolt pilots were looking forward to final victory.

FLYING OVER THE WINTER STALEMATE

Although Allied victory had not come by Christmas, the German Army Group C in northern Italy was a beaten force and Generaloberst von Vietinghoff, former commander of the 10th Army and Kesselring's replacement, knew it. XXII TAC's Thunderbolts, in conjunction with the DAF's Spitfires, had degraded the Italian rail network to such an extent that by the beginning of the New Year, the German army's supply situation had become critical, particularly in respect to food, fuel and medical supplies. An official Allied report at the time noted that 'in December alone there were 900 major breaks in those [rail] lines, only 50 of which had been repaired by the beginning of the year. Only through careful organisation of motor transport and husbanding of dwindling resources had the Germans in Italy been able to keep their logistical system from collapsing before the end of 1944'.

One of the major supplies that relied on rail transport from Germany was coal – up to 50,000 tons per month. While shipments had continued through to the end of 1944, they ceased in early January, leaving Army Group C to fend for itself. XXII TAC's Thunderbolt interdiction campaign was paying off.

Continued marginal weather throughout January limited the number of missions flown and enabled the Germans to move two full divisions out of northern Italy mostly intact. The 356th Infantry Division and the 16th SS Panzer Grenadier Division both escaped via rail through the Brenner Pass in January, being replaced by the relatively inexperienced 278th and 710th Infantry Divisions. Thunderbolts of all six groups flew when they could, but averaged only two missions per day throughout the month.

As winter dragged on, Allied and Axis forces on either side of the Apennines consolidated their positions and stockpiled those supplies that were available. On the southern side, the Allied supply situation improved significantly as materiel began flowing from Leghorn to support Fifth Army and XXII TAC – millions of gallons of aviation fuel, millions of rounds of 0.50-cal ammunition and new stockpiles of bombs, rockets and napalm.

When the weather was clear enough to fly, the focus remained on destroying rail transport and

Lts Garber and Thomas pose in front of an 86th FG P-47D at Pisa in early 1945. At this time both the 350th and 86th FGs were based here. Thomas referred to the Thunderbolt in the background as 'one of our birds, but not mine', despite the fact that no 346th FS P-47 ever had cowl rings applied like those seen on this machine (*Tyler Emery*)

anything moving behind the enemy lines. The 346th FS began the month with a successful eight-aeroplane raid on the Milan marshalling yard complex.

Prior to January, Milan had been spared from the roving fighter-bombers, and its three major marshalling yards were in somewhat better condition than those farther south. The two flights of four Thunderbolts reached Milan at 1615 hrs, attacking the marshalling yard from west to east. The first two bombs struck the west roundhouse, partially collapsing the structure and badly damaging three locomotives housed inside. The remainder of the lead flight dropped their bombs on the eastern roundhouse, destroying half of the building and four locomotives. Four more engines were severely damaged.

As the first flight pulled up, the second flight went to work, dropping its 'frag' clusters among a concentration of wagons. No fewer than 15 fully loaded cars were destroyed. The last bombs dropped took out an additional six wagons and a repair shed, and they also cut the rail line in two places.

With their bombs expended, the 346th FS pilots then made more than 30 strafing passes on each of the three marshalling yards within Milan's city limits. The day's total of 12,540 0.50-cal rounds, 12 500-lb demolition bombs and four 90-lb fragmentation clusters expended accounted for more than 70 locomotives damaged or destroyed, hundreds of wagons damaged or destroyed and a single Ju 88 at Linate/Forlanini airfield strafed and destroyed on the way home.

The next morning across the airfield from the 350th FG, a three-ship flight led by the 86th FG's deputy CO, Lt Col George Lee, took off on a ground support mission. Making contact with the 'Rover Joe' controller, Lee's flight was vectored towards Montestino to attack a company-sized force of enemy troops in the town. Each aeroplane was armed with two of the new 110-gallon napalm tanks.

Staying low to maintain the element of surprise, Lee led Capts James Covington and Vincent Relyea into the target despite intense light flak and small arms fire. All three pilots dropped their tanks precisely on target, spoiling a German counterattack against friendly infantry that were literally dug in on the opposite side of the street. After their first pass, Covington and Relyea formed back up on Lee's wing and the three P-47s came back in to make several strafing passes. Those buildings that had not been destroyed by the napalm strike crumbled under withering 0.50-cal fire from the three Thunderbolts.

Despite the success of the mission (Lee's 235th combat sortie), upon their return the 86th suspended all 'Rover Joe' operations effective 4 January 1945 until further notice. The group would only fly one additional 'Rover Joe' on the Italian front in early February before moving to a new airfield and a new theatre of operations.

While the Luftwaffe's defeat was probably most apparent to those German soldiers dug in on the Apennine peaks who had not seen a friendly aeroplane for nearly a year, there was still some life left in the Italian-based *Gruppen*.

On 20 January, while strafing enemy motor transport near Vicenza, Lt Elmer Belcher's flight of eight 346th Thunderbolts sighted an equal number of Bf 109s at 10,000 ft passing their 'three o'clock' position.

Lt Richard Sulzbach (left) had just received P-47D 44-21054 to replace his original *BUZZIN' CUZZIN'* (P-47D 42-26947), which was lost on 29 January 1945, when he got a little too eager during a strafing pass on some trucks and disregarded his airspeed and rate of descent. Pulling up just a bit too late, Sulzbach's aeroplane mushed in and flew through a grove of trees, crushing the fighter's cowling, shredding its wing leading edges and damaging the propeller, but he was able to fly the aeroplane 120 miles back to Pisa, where he then had to apologise to his irate crew chief for ruining a brand new aeroplane! (*USAF World War 2 Collection*)

The enemy formation did a half-left turn and then broke to the left, diving down on the Thunderbolt formation. Belcher turned his flight into the attack and met two of the Messerschmitts head-on. Six of the enemy fighters made their initial pass and then disengaged with a chandelle into the safety of the clouds. P-47D 42-29048 had taken a single 13 mm hit during the initial pass, but no other Thunderbolts were damaged. Belcher and his wingman, however, chased the two remaining Bf 109s. Realising that they were in trouble, the two enemy pilots split up and the two Thunderbolts followed only one of them. Belcher got a good burst in from 'six o'clock', killing the Bf 109's pilot, Tenente Enrico Brini of the *Aviazione Nazionale Repubblicana's* 2° *Gruppo Caccia*. With the exception of a few small reconnaissance units, the Messerschmitt squadrons that remained in Italy by 1945 were all part of the Fascist ANR forces.

The 346th's luck continued just over a week later. The squadron maintained an alert flight at Pisa, and on 29 January the flight was twice scrambled to intercept inbound aircraft. Both occasions turned out to be false alarms, but during the day's dusk patrol, 'Silver' flight, led by Lt Richard Sulzbach, encountered seven Ju 87s heading in a southeastly direction. 'Silver' flight had just turned back after an anticlimactic chase that had taken it more than 25 miles north of Bologna, but seeing the Stukas, the P-47 pilots were in the perfect position to attack. Mindful of the Ju 87s' rear gunners, Sulzbach led the attack and scored hits on the nearest one, seeing it go into a dive apparently out of control. Lt Clark Eddy registered good hits on another, but did not see it crash and therefore could only claim a probable. The remaining five dove for the deck, where they split up and got away. While some Ju 87s had received damage from the P-47s' guns, they managed to limp home, although their bombs had been jettisoned and their attack foiled.

While the Luftwaffe still maintained some aircraft on the Italian front, all of the fighter units that had flown in Italy had long since been pulled back to defend Germany against the constant Allied onslaught. Those units that remained were primarily reconnaissance and attack units flying a mix of Ju 87s (soon to be replaced by Fw 190Fs), Bf 109Gs, Ju 88s and Ju 188s, as well as a mix of numerous obsolete Italian types that were primarily used for night harassment raids.

With the main Allied effort sweeping into Germany, the Italian front was considered unimportant by US Strategic and Tactical Air Forces (USSTAF) HQ, and its air assets like the Twelfth Air Force were believed better used in southern France. Gen Dwight Eisenhower backed this move, which would increase the aircraft available to support his advancing armies. The MTO was seen as 'a dwindling arena of war whose chief work was done'. As a result, with the conclusion of the Malta conference between President Franklin D Roosevelt and Prime Minister Winston Churchill on 3 Feburary, it was agreed to transfer the Twelfth Air Force from Italy to southern France to support the main effort.

In the week that followed, Gen Ira Eaker, commander of the Mediterranean Allied Air Forces, did a considerable amount of

Although this P-47D of the 524th FS/27th FG was painted with the legend 1/2 *MILLION SORTIE* after Lt Irwin Lebow's flight on 8 February 1945, there was nothing special about the planning or execution of this particular 'Rover Joe' mission. The flight of four Thunderbolts had departed Pontedera at just after noon, and it had landed minus one aeroplane just before 1500 hrs (*via Osprey*)

After shutting down his P-47, Lt Lebow (third from left) poses with Maj Gen Cannon (to his right), Col DuToit (SAAF) and 27th FG CO Col Nevitt after his historic mission (*USAF World War 2 Collection*)

campaigning at USSTAF to retain tactical air assets in Italy. Moving the Twelfth to France would leave the equivalent of 12 Allied divisions without tactical air cover, and force the DAF to shift units to compensate for the lack of air power on the western half of the peninsula.

Eaker's lobbying to maintain the Twelfth in Italy worked to an extent. On the 9th USSTAF agreed that with five P-47 groups in Italy, two would immediately be shifted to the 1st TACAF (provisional) now supporting Sixth Army Group on the Franco-German border. Along with these two groups, a number of maintenance, depot and service units would be shifted as well. As a result, XXII TAC would be forced to reorganise to do more with less, but Fifth Army was able to retain its air cover. The results of this agreement would have a significant impact on XXII TAC's operations during the final months of the war in Europe.

Perhaps a deciding factor in the USSTAF agreement to leave XXII TAC in Italy was the launching of a new limited ground offensive on 8 February, codenamed Operation *Fourth Term*, by the 92nd Infantry Division. The small-scale offensive's main objective was to secure better positions from which to commence the major Fifteenth Army Group (US Fifth and British Eighth Armies) push to destroy the remaining German armies in Italy, scheduled for later in the spring.

As the 92nd advanced, P-47s from the 27th and 86th FGs coordinated with 'Rover Joe' teams to attack targets as they appeared. The 524th FS maintained a continuous presence over the frontlines throughout the day. At 1245 hrs, four 524th Thunderbolts checked in with 'Rover Joe' and were assigned three tanks in the Serchio valley as their target. When the flight reached the target area, the tanks were nowhere to be found, so the pilots were retasked with hitting the coastal guns near La Spezia to the west. These guns had been attacked repeatedly over the past several months, but continued to harass the 92nd Division's positions with intermittent artillery fire.

Lt Read, the flight leader, brought the flight in at 100 ft so as to stay undetected for as long as possible and to increase the effectiveness of the 165-gallon napalm tanks they carried – the latter were a new development of the P-38's drop tank. Aerodynamically superior to the standard 110-gallon tanks previously used by the P-47, the new Lockheed tanks also allowed for significantly more napalm to be dropped in one pass.

As the flight came in and dropped its bombs on the coastal guns, several 20 mm antiaircraft guns opened up on the flight.

Janny, P-47D 42-28063, was shot down by flak over Crailsheim, Germany, on 1 April 1945. Its pilot, Lt Laurence Nighswonger, bailed out and successfully evaded capture until he was able to link up with advancing friendly forces (*Dave Hoover Collection*)

Lt Charles Young Jr, flying on Read's wing, was hit as he came over the target. Lt Irwin Lebow, flying in the No 3 position, saw pieces fly off of Young's wing and the aeroplane roll inverted before crashing straight into the ground. Flying at an altitude of only 100 ft, Young had no chance of getting out of his stricken aeroplane. The flight's napalm tanks and guns had found their mark though, scoring two direct hits and several near misses on the coastal gun emplacements.

As the flight returned to Pontedera, its pilots were greeted by several ranking officers from the Twelfth Air Force and MAAF. Lebow, unaware of the milestone he had just achieved, shut down his aeroplane and was met by Twelfth Air Force commander Maj Gen John Cannon, Col S F DuToit of the South African Air Force and 27th FG CO Col William Nevitt. As he climbed down, Maj Gen Cannon congratulated Lt Lebow on completing MATAF's half-millionth sortie since the beginning of combat operations. While Lt Lebow and Maj Gen Cannon were talking about the mission, Lebow's crew chief hastily grabbed some black paint and painted *1/2 MILLION SORTIE* on the side of his aeroplane for the inevitable photo opportunity.

The 27th and 86th FGs continued to support the 92nd's operations, but a series of tactical blunders on the ground stymied the division and allowed the Germans to counterattack against the 370th Infantry Regiment, forcing it to withdraw or be overrun. By 10 February, the offensive had ground to a halt, despite heavy involvement by both groups' Thunderbolts. The 86th had flown 25 missions on the 8th alone, totalling 108 sorties, and the 526th had the honour of flying the group's 3000th mission. With the P-47s in the air during the day and 'Rover Joe' controllers ready to call in targets, German daytime movements were severely restricted, more than likely saving the 92nd Division from complete disaster.

As the 27th and 86th FGs returned to interdiction missions, both received orders on 11 February to prepare to move back to France to rejoin XII TAC. Within a week, the 27th was setting up operations at St Dizier airfield, in France. Two days later, the 86th arrived at Tantonville, France, and began flying combat operations over the Western Front.

The 525th FS dispersal area at Tantonville, in France, during March 1945 (*Dave Hoover Collection*)

OPERATION *ENCORE*

With *Fourth Term's* failure, it was imperative for Fifth Army to launch a new operation to secure better positions from which to launch the final offensive in April. The newly arrived 10th Mountain Division had just moved into the line and eagerly anticipated making its combat debut. The new operation, dubbed *Encore*, was to begin on 19 February and would be spearheaded by the mountain troops. They in turn had the support of the Brazilian Expeditionary Force on their right flank.

For this operation, the 57th FG was assigned as the primary air support unit for the 10th Mountain Division. The latter advanced quickly, with the 87th Mountain Infantry Regiment's 1st Battalion taking Mount Belvedere by the morning of 20 February. As the battalion was consolidating its positions on Belvedere, it came under an intense artillery barrage. Fortunately, the regiment's assigned 'Rover Joe' team was already talking to the 65th FS P-47s overhead, which quickly located and silenced the enemy guns with bombs, rockets and machine gun fire.

The Germans were at a severe tactical disadvantage with 'Rover Joe' teams in the field and 'Horsefly' aircraft overhead, and it was clear that the enemy guns were silent when aeroplanes were in the air. The 87th's war diary praised the air cover, stating 'the frontline troops came to love "Rover Joe" and Jerry was forced to keep his weapons silent while aeroplanes were overhead. The sight of the diving aeroplane, the falling bombs or flash of rockets, and the following sound of strafing or a tremendous bomb blast, was a heartening one to the soldier lying in his hole, harassed by artillery'.

Thunderbolts of the 57th continued to provide operational support through to the end of the month, but the operation was tactically complete by 22 February. *Encore* had achieved every objective through effective employment of infantry, artillery and air power in concert;

'The strongest and most coordinated counterattack the enemy seemed able to put on against our air power and superior observation was withstood on the morning of the 21st, with a very great percentage of enemy troops involved killed or captured. The enemy was proven even more unable to attack with tanks, for he couldn't even move his armour up into position under the watchful eyes of "Rover Joe". The only effective force the enemy seemed to bring on our troops was his artillery and mortar fire, and this remained heavy throughout the week.'

With the frontlines now extending almost straight across the peninsula from the Ligurian to Adriatic Seas, Fifteenth Army Group was now poised to strike the final blow on Army Group C in northern Italy.

When this photograph was taken in early March 1945, the total number of combat missions flown by these five officers (and a sixth, Maj John Dolny, who was ill at the time) totalled exactly 1000. In the front row, from left to right, are Capt Bill Colgan, CO of the 525th FS (195 missions), Lt Col George T Lee, CO of the 86th FG (245 missions), and Capt Walter Taylor of the 526th FS (119 missions), who was killed in action just a few days later while dive-bombing enemy tanks near Landau, in Germany. Sat on the wing are Capt Jesse Gore III, Ops Officer of the 86th FG (125 missions), and Capt Bushnell Welch, also of the 526th FS (189 missions), who was shot down and captured on 19 March 1945. Maj Dolny, CO of the 527th FS, had flown 127 missions by early March, raising the total for these six aviators to an even 1000 (*USAF World War 2 Collection*)

Lt James Harp's aeroplane, *Sandra*, lost power shortly after takeoff at noon on 10 January 1945. Harp jettisoned his two 500-lb bombs and was forced to belly it in a short distance from Grosseto (*64th FS collection via 57thfighter group.com/Mark O'Boyle*)

The personal mount of Maj John Dolny, CO of the 527th FS, sits ready on the edge of Pisa airfield. *Sandra Lee*, P-47D 42-26645, is equipped with a K-25 camera in the port wing pylon and has a pair of presumably empty 110-gallon napalm tanks waiting to be uploaded for its next mission (*Dave Hoover Collection*)

Sorting out the question of which unit served under what command got rather blurry with the creation of the 1st TACAF (Provisional). The 324th (Twelfth Air Force) and 50th FGs (Ninth Air Force) both remained under 1st TACAF operational control despite being assigned to different higher headquarters. In an interesting case of 'cross-pollination', this 50th FG P-47D is equipped with a K-25 tactical reconnaissance pylon-mounted camera, which was a field modification seldom seen on P-47s outside of the MTO. Indeed, the 324th FG had brought the modified P-47s into the ETO when assigned to the 1st TACAF (*Fred Schmidt via M Adamic*)

RETURN TO FRANCE

While the majority of XII TAC's Thunderbolts returned to Italy and took part in the standing up of XXII TAC and the autumn/winter campaigns of 1944, the 324th FG fought through the Vosges Mountains and on to Germany's doorstep in support of the US Seventh Army. Now, as the offensive was pushing into Germany, two additional groups were transferred back to XII TAC to give some respite to the overworked 324th. While other Ninth Air Force fighter groups had been rotated in and out of 1st TACAF to continue the northeast drive, the 50th and the 324th FGs remained at the core of the organisation's P-47 force. Although the 50th FG was a Ninth Air Force asset, it had been placed under operational control of XII TAC, and the group would remain with the command through to the end of the war.

Both groups had been at the forefront of Seventh Army's advance up the Rhone River valley, and had played a key part in the destruction of German forces at the collapse of the Colmar Pocket in early-February. While a significant portion of the German 19th Army escaped the pocket as the US 12th Armored Division and French 4th Moroccan Division met at Rouffach, in France, 1st TACAF P-47s rained almost continuous destruction on the fleeing Wehrmacht as it retreated back across the Rhine River. By the middle of the month, the US Seventh and French First Armies were preparing to cross the Rhine and enter Germany. XII TAC's Thunderbolts, however, had already been striking far into the enemy's rear.

Although a different theatre of operations, the mission profiles that the 324th flew in late 1944 through to the end of the war differed little from its XXII TAC counterparts. Interdicting rail traffic, lines of communication and enemy logistics was the 324th's primary role.

While the 27th and 86th FGs were flying in to St Dizier and Tantonville, respectively, to set up

operations, the 314th FS had a particularly successful mission on the afternoon of 22 February. Checking in with the area controller 'Baggage', no targets were available for the nine-ship flight, so it was free to attack any railway lines or communications infrastructure as desired. Eighteen 500-lb bombs were dropped on rail tracks near Bar-le-Duc, in France, making three cuts in the line. Four aeroplanes in

the formation carried rockets and they were also expended on the rails, resulting in at least one additional cut.

As the lead section was pulling up from a rocket run, the flight was bounced by 12 Bf 109s and Fw 190s from 'six o'clock high'. Lt Harry May led the counterattack, firing a long burst into the Bf 109 nearest to him. As he turned away to engage another Messerchmitt fighter, his first target exploded. May then fired at two more enemy aircraft, observing strikes and debris flying off of both, before ending his attack. As May dove into the melee, Lt John Jones scored hits on three other Bf 109s and saw pieces fall off each. All three were seen to go into uncontrolled dives, but no crashes were observed.

This low-altitude engagement ranged from ground level up to 8000 ft, and then back down again. Lt Philander Morgan fired several bursts into the wing root of another Messerschmitt, getting the squadron's second confirmed kill of the day as his foe exploded. Morgan then scored hits on another Bf 109 and an Fw 190, sending them both smoking earthward, but as neither was seen to crash they were chalked up as probables. 'Yellow' section, flying up at 8000 ft, managed to catch a solitary Fw 190 and Lts Harold Austin and Robert Hartzell combined for a probable.

As the squadron formed back up to head home to Luneville, it was discovered that Lt Nicholas Plishka's P-47 was missing. He had last been seen at 3500 ft heading west after the bomb run, prior to the dogfight. The squadron's evening report confirmed that Plishka had been killed when his aeroplane crashed four miles south of Bar-le-Duc due to unknown causes.

The 315th FS added to the 324th FG's aerial victory tally the following day when it engaged a flight of ten Bf 109s at 24,000 ft over Karlsruhe. Lt Robert Page downed a single Messerschmitt, but his wingman, Jack Rhodes, went missing after possibly being hit by flak. Rhodes was captured four miles east of Durlach, in Germany, and spent the remaining months of the war as a PoW.

With three fighter groups in each TAC, Twelfth Air Force was now evenly split between France and Italy. In France, the Luftwaffe still remained a potent, if somewhat diminished, threat, while in Italy it seemed that the enemy air arm was finished. Both commands were now able to effectively support the ground forces in their sectors while continuing the interdiction campaign that would pave the way for the final push to defeat Germany.

314th FS P-47D '39' taxis in after a mission in the spring of 1945 *Author's Collection*

When this photograph was snapped by John Haun, Lt Donald 'Pat' Patteson's P-47D *JANIE* had just started up and was preparing to taxi out on an armed reconnaissance mission (*Dave Hoover Collection*)

Lt Donald 'Pat' Patteson with his assigned P-47D, 42-27915, named *JANIE* after his wife. Patteson flew 83 missions in the Thunderbolt and also spent two weeks of detached service with Seventh Army artillery flying L-5 Sentinels (*Doug Patteson Collection*)

THE FINAL PUSH

The 27th FG returned to France on 20 February and immediately commenced supporting Seventh Army's advancing divisions and crippling German lines of communication. As the noose tightened around the Third Reich, XII TAC began seeing increased Luftwaffe activity, and the 27th's squadrons had their first opportunity since the previous summer to tangle with Reich defence units on the 25th when Lts Edus Warren Jr and William Daniel of the 523rd claimed an Fw 190 destroyed and one probably destroyed.

Three days later, while on a 12-ship bombing mission south of Karlsruhe, the 522nd FS was bounced by a mixed formation of Fw 190s and Bf 109s diving from 12,000 ft. Maj Leonard Wiehrdt was leading the 522nd's 'Green' flight, and he quickly called for the formation to jettison its bombs and belly tanks and turned to meet the attackers head-on;

'An Me 109 took a head-on pass at me and after he went by, I broke up and to the left. We were at 6000 ft then, and we started dogfighting. I continued to cut off his turn, and from that time I gained and maintained the combat advantage. I succeeded in manoeuvring to a position of 45 degrees off-stern and held a one-and-one-half radius lead until I closed to 300 yards and opened fire with a short burst. The Me started burning and the pilot pushed over and jumped out the left side.'

As Maj Wiehrdt's pilotless Messerschmitt plummeted earthwards, 'Black' flight got into the swirling dogfight and Lt James Todd turned into a near head-on pass on another Messerschmitt. Firing a quick burst at an 80-degree deflection, Todd's rounds hit home and black smoke began to trail from the Bf 109. 'I followed him down and continued to fire. At 3000 ft the pilot jumped out and I saw the 'chute open'.

The Luftwaffe had been inconsequential in shaping the battlefield as the Allied armies drove eastward across the continent. However, now that Germany was on the verge of being invaded, Wehrmacht fighters of all types became a regular sight for Thunderbolt pilots of XII TAC.

While the XII TAC was hampered by poor weather during the Colmar encirclement in early February, mid-March gave way to perfectly clear skies . Operation *Undertone* launched on 15 March with the intent of Seventh Army rolling across the Saar plain and cutting Germany off from its main source of raw materials. In conjunction with this drive, 1st TACAF focused on cutting rail lines across the region, forcing the Wehrmacht to use roads to withdraw. As in Italy, the retreat in disarray on the roads caused massive traffic jams that were easy pickings for XII TAC's P-47s. During the ten days of *Undertone*, 1st TACAF flew 12,400 sorties, the majority of which were P-47 fighter-bomber sorties.

The 314th FS had a particularly successful afternoon on 16 March, when its flight of eight P-47s contacted local controller 'Halfbake' and was vectored to a priority target in the town of Forstheim, in Alsace. Twelve German tanks were located in and around the town. Arriving overhead at 1435 hrs, the pilots were talked onto the target by a 'Horsefly' controller.

Maj Leonard Wiehrdt, one of the 27th FG's outstanding leaders and CO of the 522nd FS, shot down a Bf 109 on 28 February 1945 and met the Luftwaffe again in April, when he claimed an Me 262 damaged (*Jim Selders Collection*)

The flight's first two 500-lb bombs landed within 25 ft of one tank, badly damaging it, and the remainder (a mix of 500-lb GP and 260-lb fragmentation bombs) hit in the immediate vicinity, destroying two buildings and starting several fires. The flight, led by Lt J T Cox, then re-formed and set up a racetrack pattern, commencing a series of ten strafing passes in which ten of the tanks were either badly damaged or destroyed.

As it had done in Italy, XII TAC systematically severed the enemy's rail transport networks, effectively isolating the battlefield and restricting movement to a few avenues of retreat. Once the enemy was forced to rely on motor transport, bombing certain roads so that they were unusable allowed XII TAC to funnel the retreating enemy into choke points at the Rhine crossings, where the P-47s could maximise their destructive capabilities. The 526th's war diary entry for 21 March described the chaotic scenes in the air and on the ground as follows;

'One flight returning from a mission reported that there were so many aeroplanes bombing fleeing motor transports and enemy personnel that the flight only had time to bomb and could make no strafing passes.'

The official US Army history credits the 1st TACAF with a significant contribution to the operation's success;

'Lack of usable rail lines forced the Germans to jam the few main roads that funnelled into Germersheim, on the Rhine. Day after day, XII TAC aeroplanes relentlessly ripped and pounded at the long columns of trucks, tanks and horse-drawn carts, Claims of vehicles destroyed or badly damaged soared over the 4000 mark. The climax came on 22 March when VI Corps credited the air arm with the destruction of an entire German infantry division near Dahn.'

By the 24th the Allies were across the Rhine and advancing at breakneck speed into Germany, with an umbrella of fighter-bombers overhead. 1st TACAF realised that the end was quickly drawing near, and on 28 March an order was given that destruction of railway lines and rolling stock would no longer be the top priority target. It was believed at that point that further destruction of the rail network would be more detrimental to the Allied postwar reconstruction effort than it would to the retreating German forces. While not completely forbidden, attacks on rolling stock, marshalling yards and rail junctions dropped sharply in the coming weeks.

THE PO

In Italy, Fifteenth Army Group had consolidated its gains achieved in the limited offensives of February and gathered strength for the final offensive to push the Germans out of Italy. While the ground forces stockpiled men, materiel and ammunition for the coming campaign, XXII TAC remained diligent in keeping the north Italian rail system as motionless as possible, despite unfavourable flying conditions for a good portion of the month.

The skies were clear and visibility was unlimited on the 14th, when a 15-ship formation of 346th and 347th Thunderbolts rendezvoused with B-25s of the 321st BG en route to the target at 1045 hrs. Thirty minutes later, Lt C C Eddy, flying No 3 in Lt John Bergeron's 'Yellow' flight, spotted a formation of 16 Bf 109G-10s climbing up from Lonate aerodrome and requested permission to engage them as they were climbing. The squadron's primary mission, however, was to protect the bombers, so 'Yellow' flight continued onwards while keeping an eye out for the climbing Messerschmitts.

Periodically checking on the position of the enemy fighters, Eddy realised that they had now gained the altitude advantage and were starting to move in on the bombers. 'Yellow' flight quickly went after the Bf 109s, climbing to intercept them before they reached the friendlies. The Messerschmitts took the bait and engaged the Thunderbolts, one quickly getting a good firing position on Bergeron. A burst from Eddy's guns forced the enemy pilot to break off his attack. Roger Ellis' engine took a 20 mm cannon hit, causing him to break contact and head home, his aeroplane haemorrhaging oil. Bergeron broke away to escort Ellis home, leaving Eddy and Flt Off Walter Miller to tangle with 16 enemy machines. According to Eddy, Miller shot a Messerschmitt off of his tail, which he saw plummeting earthwards trailing thick black smoke;

'One Me, apparently the leader, decided to get things over with. He started a wingover at "two o'clock high" and came in in a steep dive. I broke into him head-on. We both started firing at long range and closed at a high rate. I saw that I was getting solid hits in his engine and wing roots. He kept firing, and as we passed within inches, I could still hear his guns. After he went by, Walt and I turned into the others.'

Although it was assumed that these were German Bf 109s, Eddy's target was the commander of 1° *Gruppo Caccia* ANR, and Italy's leading ace, Maggiore Adriano Visconti. The latter bailed out of his mortally wounded Messerschmitt and returned to fly for another month before being captured and murdered by Communist partisans. With their leader out of the fight, the remaining enemy aeroplanes broke contact and headed home while 'Yellow' flight continued its escort.

'Rhubarb', the local fighter controller, advised 'Green' flight that the disengaging Messerschmitts were headed west, and he cleared the flight to depart in pursuit. Lt Belcher's 'Green' flight, hoping to catch the bandits, headed directly for Bergamo airfield. Their gamble paid off, and Lt Robert Thompson caught a lone Bf 109 with a burst and claimed a single one damaged on the way to Bergamo. Confirmed years later by historian Ferdinando D'Amico (who has painstakingly researched the April battles between the 350th and the ANR), Thompson's claim was actually a kill, as Capitano Guido Bartoluzzi's mortally stricken aeroplane exploded on touchdown at Malpenza, killing him. Ironically, another 1° *Gruppo Caccia* Messerschmitt was destroyed at Malpenza when Maresciallo Danilo Billi's Bf 109G-10 struck the crane being used to remove the wreckage of Bartoluzzi's aeroplane from the runway. Billi was miraculously unhurt, but his aeroplane was totally destroyed.

In the meantime, 'Green' flight continued on to Bergamo and found it 'surprisingly active, with freshly painted Ju 88s and Me 109s in the dispersal area boasting orange stripes around the rear sections of the fuselage (more than likely yellow theatre ID bands)'. Belcher led Thompson, Parish and Allen down to strafe, making 15 passes over the field. When they broke off and headed home, one Ju 88 was on fire and five more, plus an SM.79 and an Bf 109, were badly damaged. Parish's 42-29304 took a 20 mm flak hit but continued on, while the flight knocked out seven 20 mm gun positions.

The Brazilians continued the airfield-busting business a week later on the 21st while on an armed reconnaissance near Milan. Their initial target was a railway repair shop, on which the four-ship flight scored a pair of direct hits with 500-lb bombs. A massive secondary explosion flattened four surrounding buildings and cut the rails adjacent to the repair facility. Off their primary target, the Brazilians turned northwest to reconnoitre the airfield at Gallarate.

Starting to run low on fuel, the four 'Jambock' (1st BFS callsign) Thunderbolts made one high pass over the airfield before coming down for a single strafing run. The initial pass sighted four SM.79s dispersed at the western end of the runway and three aircraft (two Ju 88s and an unidentified twin-engined machine) on its northern side. One of the Junkers bombers appeared to be non-operational, so the flight went after the functional SM.79s on the western side of the field, damaging three, but as none burned there were no destroyed credits given.

As the war drew closer to its inevitable end, encounters with the Luftwaffe and ANR, whether in the air or on their badly ravaged airfields, would become more frequent over both fronts. Trains, transportation and communication were now of lesser importance as the noose closed on an ever shrinking Third Reich. Airfields, or more specifically the aircraft that flew from them, were the greatest potential threat to the advancing Fifthteenth and Sixth Army Groups. With their supply lines shrunk to a minimum, the Luftwaffe did not need a large amount of fuel to deal a serious blow to US forces.

The 346th and 347th FSs each added six enemy fighters to their score over Lake Garda during another B-25 escort mission on the afternoon of 2 April, thus rendering the ANR's 2° *Gruppo Caccia* combat ineffective. Twenty-eight Bf 109s had come up to challenge the bombers, but again the 346th and 347th were 'riding shotgun' to protect the B-25s of the 57th BW. The Italians did not realise that there were two separate formations of bombers with fighter escorts flying parallel courses, and so they climbed to intercept the first bombers they saw – leading them directly into the path of the 346th, who hit them at 90 degrees deflection. The fight was on.

The 346th's Lt Richard Sulzbach drew first blood, shooting down a Bf 109 and killing Tenente Aristede Sarti. The 347th engaged a second element of Messerschmitts almost simultaneously, and within the first minute of the engagement, Capt Frank Heckencamp had sent three Bf 109s down in flames. Maj Gilbert claimed two more, while Lt Sulzbach downed one as well. The swirling maelstrom prohibited any of the Italian pilots from effectively engaging the P-47s, and when the Messerschmitts were finally able

Loaded with 110-gallon napalm tanks, two sections of 345th FS Thunderbolts head north to hit targets in the Po River valley on 6 April 1945 (*USAF World War 2 Collection*)

Lts Garber, Howard Barton and James Thomas relaxing in Pisa between missions. Barton was one of four 346th pilots to claim a kill during the 2 April shootout over Lake Garda (*Tyler Emery*)

As the air campaign's focus shifted from infrastructure and transportation denial to CAS, different types of ordnance were utilised. This 316th FS aeroplane is armed with two 500-lb M17A1 incendiary cluster bombs. The older M17A1 was not as effective as the newly developed 110- and 165-gallon napalm tanks, which had better dispersal and burned longer and hotter (*Dave Hoover*)

to disengage and retreat to fight another day, they had lost 12 of their number and not claimed a single Thunderbolt in return.

Not to be left out of the day's successes, Lts Horace Blakeney and Darwin Brooks were flying a dusk patrol for the 345th when they sighted three Bf 109s bearing down on them from about three miles out. Unknown to them, these three aeroplanes had been involved in the major air battle with the 346th, and they were now trying to get home. Dropping their belly tanks, Blakeney and Brooks turned into the inbound Bf 109s and gave chase. In the ten-minute dogfight over Verona that ensued the duo chased the three Messerschmitts through flak barrages, damaging one and forcing a second to flee. They continued to chase the third until they were able to get good hits. The pilot bailed out and the group's 13th Bf 109 of the day crashed and burned.

The lopsided victory casts the pilots of 2° *Gruppo Caccia* in a poor light. While aggressive in attempting to go after the B-25s, they underestimated the size of the P-47 escort, and as a result they were hesitant to engage, quickly losing the intiative. Many of the unit's pilots had been in combat for four years or more by this point, and these 'old hands' were simply exhausted. The newcomers, on the other hand, did not have the training or experience to mount an effective counterattack.

Forty-eight hours after the 350th's engagement over Lake Garda, the 316th FS had a very successful day over southern Germany, knocking down three German jets without loss. The day's first mission was a 12-ship armed reconnaissance, but as standard practice, Lt Mortimer Thompson checked in with ground controllers 'Baggage' and 'Baby' at 0800 hrs to see if there was a higher priority 'Pineapple' mission in their sector of responsibility. Neither controller replied in the affirmative, releasing Thompson to lead his flight on its intended mission.

Completing the first leg of their reconnoitre, the flight climbed for altitude en route to the start of its second leg. As the P-47s passed through 12,000 ft, Lt Thompson sighted a lone Arado Ar 234 twin-engined jet (most likely from 1./(F) 100) heading west about 2000 ft below his flight; 'I called a right turn and headed south just as the Ar 234 turned north. At that time I lost sight of him due to a cloud layer. A few seconds later, he appeared from beneath the clouds at the approximate position of "one o'clock low". I immediately made a right diving turn upon him. I was successful in cutting him off and got on his tail. I fired a two-second burst at close range and saw strikes enter approximately the middle of the fuselage. White smoke was seen to stream from his left nacelle. The Ar 234 then exploded, the pilot bailed out and the aircraft crashed.'

The squadron's second mission took off 15 minutes behind Lt Thompson's flight, led by Lt John Haun. On its way back from the target, the flight was attacked by four Me 262s at 9000 ft out of the sun. 'We immediately turned into the attack and they broke off,' explained Haun. 'They pulled up

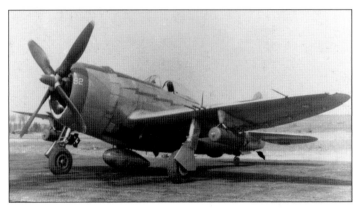

and continued making passes at us, but would not close in as long as we met them head-on. As one started to attack my section from behind, I turned into him again and started firing head-on. He started to pull up and I pulled up with him, and kept increasing my lead and firing long bursts as we closed. At the top of the pass he fell off to the left and started down in a steep dive, with heavy smoke pouring out of the fuselage.'

Haun's Me 262 was initially credited as a probable, but this was later officially changed to a confirmed kill.

The 316th's final jet kill came that evening when a flight of eight took off for the day's third armed reconnaissance mission, the P-47s loaded with 260-lb M81 fragmentation bombs. No targets were found as the flight completed its route, so Lt Andrew Kandis changed course, leading the fighters southwards toward Memmingen airfield. As the Thunderbolts roared over the airfield, a single Me 262 was spotted taking off. Quickly arming and dropping their bombs among the 30 Me 262s parked in the dispersal area, Kandis' flight attacked the slowly climbing jet. Another Me 262 entered the pattern as they started their attack, and Lt Ryland Dewey turned into it, hitting the machine with a long burst that caused a large piece of panelling to fly off the right side. Dewey's Messerschmitt recovered just before hitting the ground and managed to flee to the north, but Kandis' prey was not so fortunate;

'When I first got into position for a favourable attack, I took four ships down on him. As I got close to the aircraft, I gave him a long burst at a very close range. I saw strikes enter all parts of the aircraft, and at the same time he dropped his flaps. I made two more passes at close range, overrunning it each time, observing strikes, and on the last pass I saw pieces fly off, with a good fire going near his left wing root. The aeroplane was soon enveloped in flames and crashed on the aerodrome, being thoroughly scattered over the field.'

With German aircraft, both on the ground and in the air, now in abundance, the Thunderbolt pilots eagerly rose to the challenge. The latest D-28 and D-30 models of the P-47 were the equal of any German aircraft (bar the Me 262) they were flying against, and the American pilots were far better trained. Those experienced Luftwaffe pilots that were still flying were increasingly moved to Me 262 units like JG 7 and JV 44, where they had to learn how to fly and fight with a completely new technology that was still in its infancy. The unforgiving

Although Lt John Haun was not flying this aeroplane when he scored either of his two kills, P-47D 42-26861 *MARIE* was his assigned Thunderbolt, and the one in which he flew the majority of his combat missions. The fighter, seen here with a single kill marking beneath the cockpit, was photographed between 19 March and 4 April 1945 (*Doug Patteson*)

Lt John Haun poses in *MARIE's* cockpit (*Doug Patteson Collection*)

Towards the end of the war, XII TAC aeroplanes were actually operating from German airfields. By 18 April, the 86th FG had taken over Braunschardt, and it flew from here until well after the cessation of hostilities three weeks later. Closest to the camera is P-47D 44-33252, the 525th's '27' *Ole Baldy* assigned to Capt Jack Botten (*Author's Collection*)

The blue-painted tail identifies this as a 79th FG Thunderbolt pulling up from a strafing pass on fleeing German vehicles and troops during the final offensive to push the Wehrmacht out of Italy (*USAF World War 2 Collection*)

nature of the new jet, especially at low level and low speed, provided easy pickings for pilots of the 27th, 86th and 324th, all of whom were eager to score against the Me 262. However, on numerous occasions, many a XII TAC pilot found himself 'almost to Nuremburg before he decided the jet was too fast for him'!

Still, many claims were made against the plentiful Bf 109 and Fw 190 in the closing days of the war. On 9 April, for example, Lt Beringer Anderson of the 526th saw a flight of four Bf 109s while he was on a CAS mission and shot down two. That same day, the 527th got involved in a major 'furball', engaging Bf 109s, Fw 190s and Me 262s over Germany. Three Focke-Wulfs were destroyed and numerous others damaged both in the air and on the ground.

FINAL OFFENSIVE IN ITALY

While most of the Twelfth's fighter-bombers were dogfighting with Luftwaffe and ANR fighters over both fronts, the 57th and 79th FGs (one per field army in Fifteenth Army Group) continued to fly interdiction and CAS missions over the front in anticipation of the planned April offensive. Neither of these groups (both of whom had claimed their first German aeroplanes destroyed in 1942) would have the opportunity to engage the Luftwaffe again in air-to-air combat, but the destruction they rained down on enemy strongpoints, convoys and river and rail traffic during April 1945 was one of the key factors in the speed of the Axis collapse.

As the offensive launched on the British Eighth Army front on 9 April, both groups, along with Spitfires of the DAF, were tasked with supporting the troops' advance. The intent was to allow the Eighth Army to cross the Santerno River and establish a secure bridgehead before the US Fifth Army on the left flank began its offensive. Once the Fifth jumped off on the attack, all tactical air assets would then be assigned to cover its advance.

Targets for the initial push by IV Corps had been preplanned with XXII TAC, and a series of more than 100 artillery batteries, strong points, mortar pits and command posts were to be destroyed in the opening hours of the drive. Any road traffic in the vicinity was to be considered hostile and destroyed.

Due to weather, the offensive was delayed by two days. Finally, at 0900 hrs on 14 April, P-47s from the 57th and 79th FGs took off loaded with napalm, rockets and 'frags' to eliminate the preplanned targets. The initial focus was the area around Monte Pigna, the 10th Mountain Division's primary objective for D-Day. Frequent 'Rover' Joe calls with priority tasking came over the radio net, and as one four-ship flight expended its ordnance and headed home to refuel and rearm, another would take its place. The offensive made slow but steady progress, and the 10th Mountain and 1st Armored divisions had captured their D-Day objectives by nightfall on the 14th, albeit at a heavy price.

II Corps began its own offensive on the afternoon of the 15th, looking to quickly take ground to bring it even with IV Corps on its left. Both strategic and tactical air assets were tasked with supporting the II Corps push, MASAF flattening the area between highways 64 and 65 with hundreds of tons of high explosive, while XXII TAC's P-47s hit the area south of Bologna, focusing on Monte Sole.

'X35', a new P-47D-30, was one of the last replacement aeroplanes received by the 79th FG before war's end, and it flew combat missions in April 1945 during the final push up the Italian peninsula (*Author's Collection*)

By nightfall on 18 April it was already apparent that German resistance was failing. The 14th Army held out as best it could against the superior American firepower, but within 36 hours, the delaying action became a full blown rout, and a race between Allied divisions to see who would reach the Po River first. By the 24th, the Po had become the new Fifteenth Army Group front.

The 346th's new CO, Maj Charles Gilbert, led a four-ship consisting of Lts Martin Domin, Ray Knight and Dennis Rogers on an armed reconnaissance up the Po valley on the 23rd, and this quickly turned into another 'turkey shoot'. German vehicles were everywhere on the southern shore of the Po attempting to get across. 'I took my section to Sermide and found the roads and fields filled with enemy equipment. We split up into two elements and started to work'.

While the flight set about destroying 28 vehicles, five armoured fighting vehicles, one house and one medium tank, and damaging nearly twice that many, the enemy put up a wall of flak that eventually hit Lt Domin's P-47D 42-29028. He pulled up off of a strafing pass, rolled his aeroplane over and bailed out at roughly 1500 ft. His parachute deployed perfectly, but he did not move after hitting the ground. Domin had probably fallen victim to the intense ground fire coming up at the P-47s.

The next morning XXII TAC tasked the 346th with conducting an airfield reconnaissance patrol to check the condition of the runways at Ghedi, Villafranca and Bergamo to assess whether they could be used by Twelfth Air Force aircraft if needed. Lt Ray Knight took Lts Alva Henehan and Bill Hosey with him. Upon reaching Ghedi, it was clear that the regular pattern of depressed earth that the flight saw from the air was not filled-in bomb craters. Ghedi was mined, as was Villafranca. However, while Ghedi was otherwise quiet, something was different at the airfield. Knight had his two wingmen provide top cover while he went down to look at the runways.

It was then that Hosey saw the camouflaged aeroplanes sitting behind their revetments. Knight told Hosey to strafe them, and that he would follow. After the first pass, three aircraft were burning. By then Hosey had spotted that the style of Knight's strafing passes was different to his own. Most P-47 pilots would hit the target, break, turn outbound and then set up an inbound run back at the target. According to Hosey,

Lt Ray Knight and his crew chief, Sgt Marvin Childers, in front of Knight's assigned aeroplane, *OH JOHNNIE*. Clearly visible are the natural metal wings mated to the olive drab over neutral grey fuselage (*USAF World War 2 Collection*)

'I could also see that Knight was not attacking, going to the edge of the airfield and returning. Instead, he was attacking each revetted area then climbing steeply, rolling over and coming back down again to attack another revetted area'. Four Fw 190s, three Bf 109s and a Ju 88 had been destroyed by the time the P-47s headed back to Pisa to refuel and rearm.

Now knowing how to defeat the German camouflage, Knight was eager to get back up to Villafranca and Bergamo, positive that he knew where the aeroplanes were. His second airfield mission of the day took off at 1645 hrs when he headed for Bergamo with three other aeroplanes, bent on destruction. Knight's hunch was right and on his first pass he detonated a Ju 88 in a huge explosion, indicating that it was fully fuelled and bombs were loaded. The flight accounted for another ten Ju 88s, two Fw 190s and a single Bf 109 burning, while a P-47 took some moderate flak hits. Having expended more than half of their ammunition on the airfield and its aircraft, and with their fuel now running critically low, the P-47 pilots turned for home. Knight realised, however, that four Ju 88s had escaped the destruction, so he would have to come back to Bergamo and get them before they were able to get airborne.

On 25 April, the 346th flew its largest number of sorties, 52 in 13 separate missions, including Ray Knight's final flight. Leading 'Ivory' flight to Ghedi, Knight made sure that every aeroplane on the airfield was destroyed. Once that was confirmed, they turned for Bergamo.

Flying in low over the field, Knight immediately took fire as he cruised down Bergamo's main runway, with hits on his wing. Climbing back up to rejoin his flight, Knight ordered the pilots into line-abreast formation to maximise their forward firepower. William Rogers, flying No 3, located an aeroplane and dove on it. 'We each picked out a target and made our pass. The flak was terrific, and after getting off the field, Lt Knight called and asked if anybody was hit. Nobody was, so he then told us that he was hit badly and didn't know if the could get home or not.'

Knowing that the 350th FG was in desperate need of every available P-47, Knight elected to fly the mortally wounded fighter back to Pisa, rather than bail out. Rogers continued, 'I tried to persuade the pilot to go to Forli for a landing, as we were behind our own lines and he didn't seem to be gaining altitude. He persisted in trying to get over the mountains, so we started across below Reggio. The leader was then gaining altitude slowly, and we climbed to the last range of mountains, where I went

Lt Ray Knight climbs into the cockpit of another 346th FS aeroplane in April 1945 (*Tyler Emery*)

The carnage of defeat. Burnt out hulks of fleeing German vehicles litter the approach to a ferry crossing on the southern shore of the Po River after XXII TAC P-47s caught them in the open (*USAF World War 2 Collection*)

ahead, and then told the pilot the lowest altitude he could get through at. As I looked around, it appeared he was going to get through, but just then he hit some trees on top of the mountain. I then saw the aeroplane tumble until it struck the mountain and exploded'.

The significance of Ray Knight's airfield crusade was not immediately known, but his persistence and almost super-human accuracy were the main reason Luftwaffe bombs were not falling on Allied troops as they tried to cross the Po. A few days later, Bill Hosey signed a recommendation for a posthumous Distinguished Service Cross for Knight, but Twelfth Air Force HQ rejected it in favour of the Medal of Honor.

The Luftwaffe was still a potential threat in both Italy and Germany, even in its death throes. The 27th FG flew both B-26 escort missions and fighter sweeps over Germany during the final week of April. On the 23rd, Lt Bill Ackerman saw an Me 262 at low altitude, moving fast. Flying as No 2 in the flight, Ackerman assumed tactical lead and took the flight down to investigate;

'As we got to within 250 yards, I identified it as an Me 262. The enemy aircraft, seeing us, made a sharp turn to the right, giving me an opportunity to close within firing range. The enemy aircraft then started to climb, and I was able to get four to five good bursts from about a 15-degree angle. I observed strikes on the aircraft, causing pieces to fly off and brown smoke to issue from the fuselage. The enemy aircraft then pulled away over the clouds, and we chased it for approximately ten minutes, gradually falling behind.'

The following day, while escorting B-26s, Lts Robert Prater and John Lipiarz had similar experiences. Both pilots clearly saw their rounds impacting on the Me 262 airframes, but the jets quickly accelerated away.

Two 65th FS Thunderbolts escort a Twelfth Air Force B-25 over the ruins of an Italian marshalling yard just after war's end (*USAF World War 2 Collection*)

The group would have to wait another two days before an Me 262 was confirmed as shot down. Capt Herbert Philo was leading 'White' flight on a strafing pass on a locomotive when he saw a jet headed east roughly one mile away. Hotly pursuing the contact for nearly 15 miles, Philo closed to within 300 yards before opening fire. His first burst had no effect, so closing to 100 yards he fired again and saw pieces begin to fly off of the stricken jet. As Philo pulled up, the Me 262 began to slowly fall off to the right and then hit the ground and exploded.

The Allied seizure of the northern bank of the Po, coupled with Ray Knight's four-man onslaught that utterly obliterated the Luftwaffe strike force intended to hit the Fifteenth Army Group Po crossings, left the German high command no alternative but to surrender. The enemy's supplies had run out, their numbers depleted and those that remained were exhausted. The Germans had been utterly beaten both on the ground and in the air, and in acknowledgment of that, von Vietinghoff surrendered Army Group C on 2 May 1945, despite orders from Kesselring to the contrary.

On 4 May the 79th FG fell into formation on the beach at Cesenatico to be congratulated by Air Marshal Guy Garrod, Commander-in-Chief of RAF forces in the Mediterranean, and Air Vice Marshal R M Foster, commander of the DAF, for a job well done. With the entire group assembled, Capt Philip Bagian was supposed to lead a three-ship symbolic flyby at low-level. Bagian, who had flown 120 combat missions, was always a character, and possibly the best pilot in the 79th. He had other thoughts as to how the flyby should be performed, and made his approach on the assembled group from out over the water at near-zero altitude. Pulling up enough to sever a volleyball net near the reviewing stand as he flew by, the ceremony was promptly cut short. The war was over.

Low level! Several photographers present at the 79th FG victory formation flyby were able to capture Capt Philip Bagian's shoulder-level 'buzz job' of the beach parade ground at Cesenatico on 4 May 1945 (*Dave Hoover Collection*)

With the final link-up of Fifth and Seventh Armies near Vipiteno earlier that morning, XII and XXII TAC were once again operating in the same vicinity, although XII TAC would remain under operational control of the Ninth Air Force through to July, when it was reassigned to US Air Forces Europe. XXII TAC remained at Pomigliano until its deactivation in October, although its fighter groups quickly moved up into Germany as part of the Army of Occupation. By 8 May the cease-fire was in full effect across the continent.

The P-47 had come into the war intended as a high altitude interceptor, but through the efforts and ingenuity of the pilots and groundcrews of the Twelfth Air Force, the Thunderbolt became a true multi-role fighter. Often rivalling heavy bomb groups for bomb tonnage dropped in a single day, the six P-47 groups of the Twelfth flew hundreds of sorties on a near-daily basis for 17 months. Many times they dropped or jettisoned their bomb loads in order to engage enemy fighters, usually giving far better than they got. Thunderbolt pilots were required to fly 85, then 90, then, finally, 100 missions to complete a tour of duty.

Standing silently by, Col Leonard Lydon's personal P-47 served as the backdrop for his untimely funeral. Lydon, who was driving one of the 324th FG's assigned Jeeps, never heard a sentry's challenge as he passed a new checkpoint in Germany on 7 May 1945. The sentry, not recognising Lydon, opened fire as he passed, fatally wounding him (*Doug Patteson*)

Many pilots flew more than what was required, and many more that had returned to the US came back for additional tours. In the end, the efforts of those men proved that the outcome of the ground battle could be decisively shaped by accurate application of tactical air power, both by interdiction of enemy supply networks and through close support of friendly troops.

APPENDICES

APPENDIX A

TWELFTH AIR FORCE P-47 AIRFIELDS IN ITALY, CORSICA AND FRANCE

27th FG
Castel Volturno, Italy
Santa Maria, Italy
Ciampino, Italy
Voltone, Italy
Serragia, Corsica
Le Luc, France (25/8/44)
Salon de Provence, France (30/8/44)
Loyettes, France (11/9/44)
Tarquinia, Italy (10/44)
Pontedera, Italy (3/12/44)
St Dizier, France (22/2/45)
Toul-Ochey, France (19/3/45)
Biblis, Germany (4/45)

57th FG
Amendola, Italy
Cercola, Italy
Alto, Corsica
Ombrone (Grosseto satellite field), Italy
Villafranca di Verona, Italy
Grosseto Main, Italy

79th FG
Capodichino, Italy
Pomigliano, Italy

Serragia, Corsica
San Raphael, France (27/8/44)
Valence, France
Bron, France
Le Valon, France
Jesi, Italy
Fano, Italy
Cesenatico, Italy

86th FG
Poretta, Corsica (12/7/44)
Grosseto, Italy (17/9/44)
Pisa, Italy (23/10/44)
Tantonville, France (20/2/45)
Braunschardt, Germany (18 4/45)

324th FG
Ghisonaccia, Corsica
Le Luc, France (25/8/44)
Amberieu, France (8/9/44)
Dole-Tavaux, France (20/9/44)
Luneville, France (1/1/45)

350th FG
Tarquinia, Italy (10/9/44)
Pisa San Giusto, Italy (2/12/44)

APPENDIX B

OFFICIAL AIR-TO-AIR KILL CLAIMS BY TWELFTH AIR FORCE P-47 PILOTS

57th FG
64th FS
Paul L Carll — 14/4/44 — 2
John J Lenihan — 6/4/44 — 3
William F Nuding Jr — 23/3/44 — 1(2)

65th FS
Ivan U Andrus — 29/1/44 — 1
Richard O Hunziker — 12/1/44 — 1(1)
Philip M Miholich — 12/1/44 — 1

66th FS
Stephen L Bettinger — 1/7/44 — 1
William C Clark — 14/1/45 — 1
Howard W Cleveland — 1/7/44 — 2
Thomas D Davis Jr — 1/7/44 — 1
William H Ehney — 25/5/44 — 1
Edwin O Flood — 25/4/44 — 1
Walter H Henson — 14/3/44 — 1

Richard L Johnson — 1/7/44 — 1
Robert E Kaiser — 25/5/44 — 1
George Kriss — 25/5/44 — 2(1)
Claude G Rahn — 1/7/44 — 1
Warren L Shaw — 17/12/43 — 1(1)
Donald A Smith — 24/3/44 — 1

27th FG
522nd FS
Gary A Theodore — 12/8/44 — 1
Herbert A Philo — 26/4/45 — 1
James R Todd — 28/2/45 — 1
Leonard L Wiehrdt — 28/2/45 — 1
Robert E Williams — 6/2/45 — 1

523rd FS
William W Daniel — 25/2/45 — 1
George W Holmquist — 29/1/44 — 1
Randall L Jones — 11/4/45 — 1

Harry H Moreland	12/4/45	1
Maurice E Ruby	23/4/45	1
Edus H Warren Jr	25/2/45	1

524th FS

Clyde F Brown	26/5/44	1

79th FG

85th FS

Charles W Defoor Jr	17/3/44	1
Raymond L Higgins	7/2/44	1
Earl P Maxwell	5/9/44	1
Carl W Stewart	17/3/44	1(1)

86th FS

Robert L Crawford Jr	13/5/44	1
George W Ewing Jr	13/7/44	1
Jack C Fortune	9/9/44	1
Charles T Hancock	26/7/44	2
Malcolm F Hayles	13/5/44	1
Billy M Head	26/7/44	2
Richard W Hilgard	26/7/44	1
Robert L Pepper	13/5/44	1

87th FS

Damon E Adkins	15/5/44	1
Ronald M Faison	24/9/44	1
Walter G Petermann	15/5/44	1

86th FG

525th FS

Henry Aegerter Jr	7/4/45	1
Marion L Green	7/4/45	1

526th FS

Beringer A Anderson	9/4/45	2
Bert Benear	19/8/44	1
Roy W Brown Jr	27/4/45	1
James R Gloeckler	24/4/45	1
Alfred E Ireland Jr	24/4/45	1
Paul Moody	27/4/45	1

527th FS

Jesse R Core III	10/12/44	1
Doyle W Hastie	9/4/45	0.5
Carl E Hefner	9/4/45	0.5
George E Hill	1/12/44	1
Allan A Leventhal	9/4/45	0.5
Leonard D Milton	9/4/45	1.5

324th FG

314th FS

Harold Austin	22/2/45	0.5
Alpheus F Berlin	25/12/44	0.25
Kenneth E Dahlstrom	25/12/44	0.25
Harry C May Jr	22/2/45	1
George V McClintic	9/4/45	1
Joseph A Miller	9/4/45	1
Philander D Morgan Jr	22/2/45	3
William C Potter	9/4/45	0.5
Glenn R Putt	25/12/44	1.5
Oscar W Sparks	26/11/44	1
James L Spencer	9/4/45	0.5
Robert C Stickell	25/12/44	0.25

315th FS

Jack T Hasling	9/4/45	1
Paul G Long	9/4/45	1
Robert L Page	23/2/45	1
Herman F Pilsbury	9/4/45	1

316th FS

Wilbur G Allen	22/12/44	1
Ryland T Dewey	22/12/44	1
Edwin H Harley	24/3/45	1
John W Haun	19/3/45 and 4/4/45	2
Andrew N Kandis	4/4/45	1
Frank E Pardue	22/12/44	1
Alvin D Prusia	17/12/44	1
William R Richmond Jr	22/12/44	1.5
Clarence B Slack	22/12/44	1.5
Mortimer J Thompson	4/4/45	1

350th FG

345th FS

Horace W Blakeney	2/4/45	0.5
Darwin G Brooks	2/4/45	0.5

346th FS

Howard L Barton	2/4/45	1
John E Bergeron	14/3/45	1
James B Dailey Jr	31/10/44	1
Charles C Eddy	2/4/45	1
Charles E Gilbert II	2/4/45	2
Walter R Miller	14/3/45	1
Richard P Sulzbach	2/4/45	2
Robert C Tomlinson	31/10/44	2(1)

347th FS

Sigmund E Hauser	3/3/45	1
Frank W Heckenkamp	2/4/45	3
Edward M Olson	2/4/45	1
James H Young	23/2/45	1

Note

Parentheses indicate kills scored in different airframes

COLOUR PLATES

1
P-47D-15 42-75648 of Lt Al Froning, 65th FS/57th FG, Amendola, Italy, February 1944

Although 42-7568 was not the aeroplane in which he scored his final two kills, Al Froning had it marked up with all six of his victories. The fighter replaced the P-47D-4 that was nearly shot out from under him in the 57th FG's first engagement flying the Thunderbolt. Although Froning's aeroplane was damaged by cannon fire, he in turn used it to shoot down two Bf 109s, thus becoming the first Twelfth Air Force pilot to score aerial victories in the Thunderbolt. Although Froning made no claims in this aeroplane, on 11 January 1944 he used it to drive several Bf 109s off the tails of his squadronmates. White '51' was one of the first 65th FS aeroplanes to be modified with the Wymond/Hahn bomb release system.

2
P-47D-15 42-75820 *The Wog* of Lt Stan 'Luigi' Morrow, 65th FS/57th FG, Alto, Corsica, summer 1944

One of several garishly painted Thunderbolts from the 65th FS's C Flight, *The Wog* was flown by Lt Stanley 'Luigi' Morrow during the summer of 1944 from Corsica over both Italy and southern France. With the operational pace at this time, it was often difficult to paint pin-up artwork on P-47s in the MTO. As a quick solution to add some colourful pin-ups to their aeroplane, Morrow and his crew chief took pages directly out of the 1944 Varga calendar and shellacked them to the side of the Thunderbolt! *The Wog* carried no less than four Varga pin-ups into battle, along with an expertly rendered Disney 'Big Bad Wolf'.

3
P-47D-23 42-27683 *"JEETER"* of Lt Col William 'Jeeter' Yates, Deputy CO of the 57th FG, Grosseto, Italy, December 1944

Col Yates was one of the original 57th FG pilots, being the 16th aviator to fly a P-40 from the deck of USS *Ranger* to Accra, on the African Gold Coast, on 19 July 1942. After a tour stateside, he returned to the group as its deputy commander in the spring of 1944. Yates' assigned aeroplane, 42-27683 was one of four lost by the 66th FS on 9 December 1944 over northern Italy. Yates finished the war with two shared victories to his name – a quarter and a half credit for Bf 109s destroyed in late 1942 while flying P-40Fs in North Africa with the 66th FS.

4
P-47D-26 42-28307 *"TOOTS"/"LIL'ABNER"* of Lt Joseph Angelone, 66th FS/57th FG, Grosseto, Italy, October 1944

Heading out on a mission over the Po River valley on 7 October 1944 in this aircraft, Lt Joseph Angelone had a tyre blowout at 100 mph while taking off from Grosseto. The fully laden Thunderbolt lacked sufficient airspeed to fly, and as the centre of gravity shifted, the aeroplane swerved into a mound of earth adjacent to the runway and nearly flipped over. Its right main gear snapped, digging the wingtip into the earth and upending the entire aeroplane. Fortunately, the momentum did not carry it all the way onto its back. Angelone jumped out as fuel from the ruptured fuselage and auxiliary tanks ignited, quickly enveloping the entire aeroplane in a huge fireball. The fighter was a complete loss, while Angelone walked away with minor bruises. The pilot's next P-47, also a 'Dash 26', was similarly marked and carried the number '71' on it through to the end of the war.

5
P-47D-27 42-27179 *Sandra* of Lt James Harp Jr, 64th FS/57th FG, Grosseto, Italy, January 1945

Assigned to 2Lt James Harp Jr, this particular Thunderbolt lost power shortly after takeoff on 10 January 1945 and Harp wrestled the uncooperative aeroplane back to Grosseto Main. Jettisoning his bombs over the sea, he brought *Sandra* in for a belly landing, crushing the wingtip and underside and badly damaging the engine. Harp was one of the 17 pilots assigned to the 64th FS at the time, and he earned a Distinguished Flying Cross for the 4 March 1945 mission where he took significant flak damage over the target, but still managed to bring his stricken fighter back to Grosseto before bailing out safely over the field.

6
P-47D-30 (serial unknown) of Col Gladwyn Pinkston, CO of the 79th FG, Cesenatico, Italy, April 1945

Col Pinkston served as Deputy Operations Officer for XXII TAC until assuming command of the 79th FG on 28 November 1944. He flew 97 combat missions over Italy, France and Yugoslavia during his tour with the group. Pinkston had earned his wings in 1938 as an Aviation Cadet at Kelly Field, Texas, and served his first assignment flying P-26 Peashooters with the 18th Pursuit Group at Wheeler Field, Hawaii.

7
P-47D-20 42-25274 *PISTOL PACKIN MAMMA* of Lt Richard Long, 85th FS/79th FG, Pomigliano, Italy, May 1944

Lt Long joined the 79th FG in the spring of 1944, and by May he had already become an accomplished aviator. He flew this aeroplane in the 85th FS engagement on 1 July against Bf 109s most likely from JG 77 – Long claimed a shared credit with Lt Cecil Bush in the damaging of a Messerschmitt. Like Stan Morrow's *The Wog* from the 57th, Long admired two of the 1944 Varga calendar pin-ups enough to affix them to the side of his aeroplane. He flew 109 combat missions with the 85th FS and completed his combat tour in October 1944.

8
P-47D-40 (serial unknown) of the 85th FS/79th FG, Cesenatico, Italy, April 1945
One of the last replacement P-47s issued to the 79th FG prior to the cessation of hostilities, this aeroplane saw some limited combat in the closing weeks of the war, and remained on hand into the occupation period. It is uncertain why the code number was painted red, rather than the regulation black. Several photographs of this aeroplane exist showing both wartime markings and postwar red/yellow/red 'Occupation bands' in early 1946.

9
P-47D-28 (serial unknown) *DEACON DANDY* of the 86th FS/79th FG, Fano, Italy, February 1945
This late model D-28 was seen at Fano in February 1945, loaded with 110 gallon napalm tanks and rocket tubes, waiting for a mission over the Eighth Army front. When the 27th, 57th, 79th and 86th FGs returned to Italy from Corsica, all four were initially under operational control of the British DAF. However, just a few weeks later with the creation of XXII TAC, all but one group returned to USAAF control. The 79th, however, remained with the DAF until the cessation of hostilities. By 19 February 1945, the weather had improved after a long and bleak winter, allowing the 86th FS to resume its campaign against German transport and rail traffic along the Yugoslavian coast.

10
P-47D-27/28 (serial unknown) *ANGELPUSS II* of Lt Louis Barnett, 86th FS/79th FG, Fano, Italy, March 1945
2Lt Robert Hewitt was killed in Louis Barnett's original *ANGELPUSS* (a P-47D-21) when it went down during a combat mission over Bodres, in Italy, on 21 January 1945. With the mission tempo only increasing in the closing months of the war, the 86th FS was quickly issued a replacement aeroplane in the form of this 'bubble-top' D-28 that was christened *ANGELPUSS II*. Barnett completed his tour, the majority of his missions flown in this aeroplane through to the cessation of hostilities.

11
P-47D-15 42-75671 of the 87th FS/79th FG, Serragia, Corsica, July 1944
One of the first aeroplanes in the group to get the outfit's new blue tail, 'X73' flew from Serragia during the lead-up to Operation *Dragoon* and after. Although not a widely adopted practice, 'X73' had the last three digits of its serial painted just ahead of the empennage. This 'Skeeters'' aeroplane is seen carrying two 500-lb GP bombs and a 75-gallon centreline external tank to increase its loiter time over the French Riviera. With nearly 200 miles to travel across the Mediterranean, by D+3 (18 August)

all P-47s flying over southern France stopped carrying bombs and began carrying a load of three 75-gallon drop tanks just to give them the endurance to support rapidly advancing friendly units.

12
P-47D-25 42-26444 *Candie Jr.* of Lt Robert Hosler, 522nd FS/27th FG, Pontedera, Italy, December 1944
42-26444 was the assigned aircraft of 1Lt Robert Hosler, and on 10 September 1944 he flew it on an armed reconnaissance mission with his unit to Freiburg, in Germany. As flight lead, Hosler sighted a moving train loaded with artillery and motor transport. Leading the P-47s in an attack, he personally destroyed the locomotive and set fire to 12 freight wagons. Pulling up from the first train, the flight then strafed several additional trains and a troop concentration until their ammunition was all but exhausted. This particular aircraft was destroyed in a taxiing accident on 6 December 1944, and Lt Hosler began flying *Candie Jr. II* shortly thereafter following his promotion to squadron operations officer. Although 42-26444 is a D-25 model, this particular aeroplane flew with at least two different types of Curtiss propeller during its combat career.

13
P-47D-30 44-20856 *BETTY III* of 1Lt Robert Jones, 522nd FS/27th FG, Heilbronn, Germany, 2 April 1945
As Seventh Army pushed further into Germany, the 27th FG provided CAS and armed reconnaissance for the advancing elements on a regular basis. On 2 April 1945, during an eight-ship reconnaissance over Heilbronn, Germany, the 522nd FS located and attacked an artillery position. Lt Robert Jones was flying as 'Yellow 3' in this aircraft. While on his gun run, intense and accurate light flak opened up on the flight and Jones' *BETTY III* was seen to take several hits. According to his wingman, 2Lt James Snellbaker, the aeroplane climbed up into the overcast, and that was the last the flight saw of him. The wreck was located two weeks later and Jones' body recovered after the 100th Infantry Division liberated Heilbronn.

14
P-47D-27/28 (serial unknown) of Lt Irwin Lebow, 524th FS/27th FG, Pontedera, Italy, 8 February 1945
Lt Lebow flew as No 3 in a four-ship 'Rover Joe' mission in support of the 92nd Infantry Division on 8 February 1945. Originally tasked with knocking out three tanks just north of the bomb line, Lebow's flight was unable to locate them and was retasked with dropping their napalm canisters on the coastal artillery guns at La Spezia instead. The flight was on-target, but lost Lt Charles Young to flak on the bomb run. On their return, Lebow was informed that he had just flown the half-millionth sortie for the Twelfth Air Force. His crew chief hastily painted *1/2 Million Sortie* on the side of the aeroplane for the photo opportunity with

Twelfth Air Force commander Maj Gen Cannon at Pontedera. While the aeroplane did not feature this legend on its fuselage side during the mission, the P-47 is depicted here carrying the new 165-gallon napalm tanks that the flight had expended.

15

P-47D-28 42-28604 *DORA PAT III* of Lt Col George Lee, deputy CO of the 86th FG, Pisa, Italy, October 1944

Lt Col Lee came to the 86th FG in the autumn of 1944, having flown 191 combat missions with the 79th FG since North Africa. Lee was serving as the commander's of the 87th FS when he was transferred to the 86th to assume the deputy commander position. Lee would go on to fly another 67 missions as deputy CO and then CO of the 86th FG. Promoted to full colonel at the age of just 25, he was one of the youngest officers in the USAAF to attain this rank. 42-28604 was lost on 3 October 1944 during a strafing mission over Villafranca aerodrome, its pilot, Lt Richard Oldham, being killed.

16

P-47D-30 44-20863 *Lois* of Lt John Brink, 525th FS/86th FG, Grosseto, Italy, 25 December 1944

On Christmas Day, Lt Brink led an eight-ship mission to attack a railway bridge near Nervesa, in Italy. Although the flight encountered marginal weather en route to the target, Lt Brink led the flight precisely to the target. All eight aircraft registered hits or near misses on the bridge, badly damaging it. The approaches and tracks were also blown up. As the flight pulled off the target, they dropped down to strafe rolling stock in the area. Lt Brink and his flight destroyed or damaged eight locomotives, three wagons, more than 20 motor vehicles of various types, three tanks and a number of gun positions. For his outstanding leadership, Brink was awarded the Distinguished Flying Cross for this mission.

17

P-47D-23 42-28132 *VIV'S BABY SHOES* of Lt Bill Goslin, 527th FS/86th FG, Corsica, September 1944

Named for Lt Bill Goslin's infant daughter, *VIV'S BABY SHOES* served as his assigned aircraft from July 1944 until he was forced to ditch it in the Ligurian Sea after it was damaged by flak on 12 September. Goslin managed to nurse his stricken aeroplane back to the coast from the Po valley, but he then had to ditch it when the engine seized after running out of oil. Stopping to try and pry the clock out of the instrument panel as a keepsake, Goslin stayed with his aeroplane until it sank. He was quickly picked up by an RAF search and rescue launch. Returned to the 527th FS that evening, Goslin was back on flight status within the week. He eventually completed his 90-mission tour of duty.

18

P-47D-25 42-25645 *Sandra Lee* of Maj John Dolny, 527th FS/86th FG, Tantonville, France, January 1945

Since the only USAAF tactical reconnaissance squadron available in-theatre had continued through southern France with XII TAC, XXII TAC Thunderbolt units soon found a new role – providing photographic reconnaissance imagery to battlefield commanders. Although it is uncertain which group created the new modification, it was in use operationally with every Twelfth Air Force P-47 unit by the end of hostilities. The system consisted of a K-25 camera mounted in the leading edge of the aeroplane's left underwing pylon that was operated via a control switch wired into the cockpit. Thunderbolts with this modification suffered no degradation in performance and still carried full bomb loads, allowing them to shoot photographs of their targets.

19

P-47D-27 42-27000 of Col Leonard Lydon, CO of the 324th FG, Luneville, France, March 1945

Col Lydon assumed command of the 324th in December 1943, and he led the group through the P-47 transition to the end of the war. Lydon scored his only kill while flying a P-40F on 15 December 1943, just after he assumed command of the group. Admired and respected by his men as a dynamic leader, he began his career with the 57th Pursuit Group prior to the US entry into World War 2. Fighting through North Africa, and prior to taking command of the 324th, Lydon briefly commanded the Fifteenth Air Force's 325th FG. Tragically, he was accidentally shot and killed by an American sentry while driving in his Jeep just after the cessation of hostilities in Italy on 7 May 1945.

20

P-47D-27 42-27105 of Lt Stan Hart, 314th FS/324th FG, Ghisonaccia, Corsica, August 1944

Lt Stan Hart had just had '36' assigned as his personal aircraft when Operation *Dragoon* commenced in August, 1944. On the evening of D-Day for the invasion of southern France, the 314th FS was sent to strafe Les Chanoines airfield in an effort to destroy the Luftwaffe's ability to counterattack the invasion fleet by air under the cover of darkness. The 12-ship mission dead-reckoned nearly 300 miles from Ghisonaccia, on Corsica, and found its target just as the summer sun was setting. Lt Hart was flying No 4 in the lead flight of four, and as it dropped down on the deck, two Ju 88s on the ground loomed into his sights. Hart opened fire, kicking his rudder back and forth for maximum coverage. His rounds found their mark on both Junkers bombers, but neither exploded or 'flamed up'. As a result, Hart was given credit for two Ju 88s damaged.

21

P-47D-27 42-27277 *MISS ANN* of Lt Richard Keene, 315th FS/324th FG, Luneville, France, March 1945

When 1Lt Richard Keene was forced to belly land *MISS ANN* in a field near Seventh Army's frontlines due to a runaway prop on 21 March 1945, it was the second time in three months that 42-27277 had endured a hard landing – Keene was picked up by elements of the 7th's Signals

Battalion. Originally assigned to the 314th FS as *Amy Lou*, and wearing side number '37', the fighter had suffered a landing accident at Luneville on 9 January 1945 with Capt Harry Chance at the controls.

22
P-47D-25 42-26861 *MARIE* of Lt John Haun, 316th FS/324th FG, Germany, 4 April 1945

Lt John Haun scored his two kills in the closing months of the war, when encounters with the Luftwaffe were becoming more common. By March 1945, the 324th was operating over the Third Reich with impunity, continuing the disruption of communication lines, railway lines and motor transport across southern Germany. The 316th FS had one of its most successful days on 4 April when no less than four German jets were brought down by 'Hell's Belles'' guns. Lt Haun was leading 'Blue' section on the way back from an eight-ship dive-bombing mission when it was attacked by four Me 262s. 'Blue' section turned in to their attackers and Haun opened fire head-on. The jet fell away to the left and headed down in a steep dive, with smoke pouring from the fuselage. The Messerschmitt disappeared into the clouds, so initial confirmation was difficult and Haun was credited with a probable. However, a few days later the jet's wreckage was located and his second kill was confirmed. Haun scored both of his kills in head-on attacks, bringing down an Me 262 and a Bf 109. The two Me 262s and two Ar 234s claimed by the 316th on 4 April were a significant portion of just a handful of jets credited to P-47 pilots in the final weeks of the war in Europe.

23
P-47D-23 42-27915 *JANIE* of Lt Donald 'Pat' Patteson, 316th FS/324th FG, Dole-Tavaux, France, January 1945

When Donald Patteson arrived at the 316th FS in November 1944, he had already been a flight instructor for two years, and had more than 2200 hours in single-engined and 150 hours in twin-engined aircraft in his logbook. His combat career got off to an exciting start when the squadron tangled with the Luftwaffe over Bad Wurttemburg on only Patteson's second combat mission. He was assigned veteran P-47D-23 42-27915 shortly thereafter, and he named it *JANIE* after his wife. As an experienced pilot coming into the unit, Patteson quickly became a flight leader, and he completed his tour having flown 83 combat missions in the P-47. In addition to his Thunderbolt combat missions, Patteson spent ten days of detached service with the Seventh Army Artillery flying a Stinson L-5 'Horsefly' on spotter missions over the front.

24
P-47D-27 42-27260 *FLAK HAPPY* of Lt H L Sumner, 345th FS/350th FG, Pisa, Italy, April 1945

The *FLAK HAPPY* artwork adorned both sides of this P-47D-27's cowling when it flew more than 200 combat sorties with the 345th FS in 1944-45. On 6 April 1945, 42-27260 took part in an eight-ship dive-bombing mission against a supply depot in the Po valley. The flight dropped all of its 110-gallon napalm tanks on target, setting both it and the surrounding woods on fire. Returning to make two strafing passes, the flight attacked a small building in the valley that unexpectedly exploded, indicating its possible use as an ammunition or fuel storage facility. It is unclear whether *FLAK HAPPY* had a regularly assigned pilot, but records indicate that it was routinely flown by several of the 345th's pilots, including Lt Sumner.

25
P-47D-25 42-26947 *BUZZIN' CUZZIN'* of Lt Richard Sulzbach, 346th FS/350th FG, Pisa, Italy, 29 January 1945

The first of two aeroplanes with this name assigned to Richard Sulzbach, *BUZZIN' CUZZIN'* was so named after a failed attempt in December 1944 to buzz the 350th's pilot's quarters in Pisa. On 29 January 1945, leading 'Silver' flight on the daily dusk patrol from Pisa, Sulzbach shot down a Ju 87 of NSGr 9 while flying this aeroplane. 42-26947 remained his assigned P-47 until 30 March 1945, when it failed to return from a mission whilst being flown by Lt Glenn Parish. Scheduled to lead a dive-bombing and armed reconnaissance mission, Parish and his flight bombed their primary target and then turned towards La Spezia. The flight subsequently made several passes on an ammunition dump, to some minor effect. However, on his third pass, Parish's rounds caused a massive explosion and fireball that billowed up to 3000 ft, enveloping his aeroplane. The dump had been completely obliterated, but at cost of Parish and 42-26947.

26
P-47D-25 42-26785 *OH JOHNNIE* of Lt Ray Knight, 346th FS/350th FG, Pisa, Italy, 25 April 1945

Lt Ray Knight flew through his own bomb blast on a January 1945 dive-bombing mission, necessitating a wing replacement on his trusted mount. Knight's aeroplane was the only olive drab-painted P-47 in the 350th FG, and it was most likely earmarked for the 1st BFS before being assigned to the 346th FS. Knight was a gifted pilot, and he was quickly made a flight leader after joining the group. Specialising in low-level strafing attacks, he led several strikes on German airfields in the last weeks of the war, personally destroying or damaging more than 20 enemy aircraft. To support the Fifth Army drive to the Po, the 346th needed every one of its aeroplanes to be mission capable, and despite serious damage to his P-47, Knight elected to fly his stricken fighter back to Pisa rather than bail out. However, when crossing the Apennines, his Thunderbolt became more difficult to control and as he tried to belly land, Knight's wing hit a tree, causing the aeroplane